D1556906

Death of the Chesapeake

Scrivener Publishing
100 Cummings Center, Suite 541J
Beverly, MA 01915-6106

Publishers at Scrivener
Martin Scrivener (martin@scrivenerpublishing.com)
Phillip Carmical (pcarmical@scrivenerpublishing.com)

Death of the Chesapeake

A History of the Military's Role in Polluting the Bay

Richard D. Albright

Scrivener
Publishing

WILEY

Co-published by John Wiley & Sons, Inc. Hoboken, New Jersey, and Scrivener Publishing LLC, Salem, Massachusetts.
Published simultaneously in Canada.

For general information on our other products and services or for technical support, please contact our Customer Care Department within the United States at (800) 762-2974, outside the United States at (317) 572-3993 or fax (317) 572-4002.

Wiley also publishes its books in a variety of electronic formats. Some content that appears in print may not be available in electronic formats. For more information about Wiley products, visit our web site at www.wiley.com.

For more information about Scrivener products please visit www.scrivenerpublishing.com.

Cover design by Russell Richardson

Library of Congress Cataloging-in-Publication Data:

ISBN 978-1-118-68627-0

Printed in the United States of America

10 9 8 7 6 5 4 3 2 1

Dedication

This book is dedicated to my wife Sheila, my helmsman Arie Albright and my sonar operator and navigator Richard Albright II.

It is also dedicated to Granville Albright, and the crew of the U.S.S. Sea Cat. The Sea Cat operated in the Yellow Sea in water too shallow to submerge her periscope. In so doing she denied the enemy a previously unchallenged supply shipping lane, sinking much tonnage. The Sea Cat was honored by being invited to attend the surrender of Japan in Tokyo Bay.

Contents

Preface

In essence this book deals with an area that contributes significantly to the pollution and degradation of Chesapeake Bay, but has been completely overlooked in many of the efforts to restore the Bay, specifically, the federal pollution sources. The book also stresses, perhaps for the first time, that efforts to restore the Bay have failed because of violation of a fundamental precept of environmental cleanup: that is, to sample the site and see what is there. The Bay itself has never been sampled.

Thus this book presents a view of the environmental condition of Chesapeake Bay that is totally unique. It covers a part of the history of the Bay that is not widely known, including how the Bay was formed. It presents a mixture of science, military history, intriguing travel sights, warnings, and novel solutions to the Bay's degradation. It dispels some long-held views on the geology and environmental issues of the Bay. Hopefully, it will provide an easily understood and enjoyable reading adventure for those with an interest in the Bay itself, whether boater, seafood fancier, historian, veteran, environmentalist, fishing enthusiast, or adventurist.

One of the most challenging tasks in writing this book was deciding how to arrange the material into chapters and subparts. Since the book deals with four classes of environmental contaminants that have been overlooked, the toxic effects of each are presented separately. Some of the arrangement is geographical, such as following a river downstream and naming the main military facilities along the way.

Rivers, however, can cross state lines and county lines. Thus it is difficult to simply figure out the impacts from a particular reader's political subdivision or locale, let alone to their favorite fishing spot.

Some of the arrangement is by ordnance type or delivery system. An effort was made to separate out bombing ranges, artillery ranges and mined areas, assuming a particular reader may only be interested in a particular ordnance type, delivery system, branch of service, or area with navigational hazards.

Ranges were separated from explosive and gunpowder manufacturing facilities as these produced much more pollutants than some static firing areas.

Finally, chemical weapons facilities, radioactive disposal sites, and Polychlorinated Biphenyls (PCBs) were separated since such contaminants pose different safety and health risks from explosives.

An effort was made to deal with the differing environmental effects from explosives, chemical weapons, and other contaminants present on individual military sites.

Explosive and gunpowder manufacturing facilities were also separated as these produced much more pollution than static firing areas.

If that doesn't make sense, in the author's defense, the Chesapeake Bay is a large multi-state area impacted by a vast network of rivers and streams, municipalities, and air pollution sources with an intriguing, active and complicated history. Military facilities may have more than one type of ordnance or be involved with more than one principle contaminant.

Washington, D.C
April 2013

Special Recognition for Those Who Enlightened the Author on Underwater Issues or on the Chesapeake Bay Itself

Non-fictional books covering complicated subject matter are often based on more knowledge than one individual possesses. This is especially true when several different areas of expertise are involved. *The Death of the Chesapeake* involves many disciplines; history, geology, environmental science, military science, navigation, conventional and chemical ordnance, and other subjects all set in one of the world's largest and most important estuaries. Accordingly, the author is indebted to many people whose knowledge is intrinsically woven in these pages.

Although every effort was made to offer the citations and quotations for ideas or facts presented, one does not always remember where this or that idea or fact came from when writing an extensive book, and so the author apologizes for any omissions of credit. Some individuals contributed so substantially to the author's interest and knowledge that they bear special mention.

James Barton, USN Retired Navy Seal and inventor of an underwater ordnance harvester. Ten years ago, when the author first began to appreciate the issues of underwater ordnance, Jim was his primary mentor and still is the author's go-to person. Jim has provided some of the photographs in the book and the sidescan sonar unit used in the author's research.

Reporters John Bull, Matthew Sturdevant, and Stephanie Heinatz. These individuals are ahead of the pack in appreciating and reporting on the munitions issues in the Bay. Knowledge gained from their work both motivated the author to write this book and added to the completeness of the manuscript.

Robert Johnson, MD, worked with the author on the environmental aspects of military munitions sites and was an early environmental researcher on Chesapeake Bay dumpsites and ordnance constituents. He contributed a chapter for the book.

Terry Klump, the best dive partner the author ever had. Terry and the author explored the underwater world in Lake Huron. Terry introduced the author to the Ann Arbor Amphibians Dive Club, one of whose members, Bill, was personal friends with Cousteau. Whenever Cousteau would come to the Great Lakes area, he would stay at Bill's house and the club would be invited to see movies of his latest dives, usually in the Mediterranean. Cousteau, of course, introduced the author to the concept of environmental protection of the underwater world.

Rickey Stauber is an ordnance expert and archival researcher. Many of the brave ordnance and demolition (EOD) experts in the country probably took a class or two from Mr. Stauber or at least their instructors did. Rickey Stauber is one of the unsung heroes in the 9/11 attack on the Pentagon. The plane hit near where he worked and he helped to rescue several people and then fought numerous fires with hand-held extinguishers until the fire department was able to enter.

Terry Slonecker, PHD, an expert in remote sensing, was deeply involved in assessing the potential environmental issues of some of the sites mentioned in this book.

Lenny Siegel has directed an environmental group which studies military contaminants among other things. He and his organization have written numerous scientific papers on contaminants of concern and munitions issues.

John Fairbank is a Maryland Department of Environmental Quality professional who specialized in Formerly Used Defense Site (FUDS) issues. He has always provided inspiration to the author and been a stalwart defender of the environment.

List of Acronyms

DIN	Dissolved Inorganic Nitrogen
DNA	Dioxyribonucleic Acid (The basic genetic material in all living things)
DM	Adamsite
DMA	A Methylated Arsenical
DNB	Dinitrobenzene
DNT	Dinitrotoluene
DO	Dissolved Oxygen
EOD	Explosive Ordnance Disposal
FUDS	Formerly Used Defense Site
GA	Tabun (a nerve agent)
GB	Sarin (a nerve agent)
GD	Soman (a nerve agent)
GPS	Global Positioning System
HBX	High-Explosive made from TNT, RDX, Aluminum, Lecithin, and Wax
HMX	High Melting Explosive
IHD	Ischemic Heart Disease
MMA	A Methylated Arsenical
MSX	Multinucleate Sphere X (disease in oysters)
NAS	Naval Air Station
NDMA	Nitrodisodamethylamine
NRL	Naval Research Laboratory
PCB	Polychlorinated Biphenyl (electrical insulating oil)
PETN	Pentaerythritoltetranitrate
POTW	Publicly Owned Treatment Works
RDX	Royal Demolition Explosive

TN	Total Nitrogen
TNA	Tetranitroanaline
TNB	Trinitrobenzene
TNT	Trinitrotoluene
TP	Total Phosphorus
TRI	Toxic Release Inventory
UUV	Unmanned Underwater Vehicle
VX	O-Ethyl S-2-diisopropylaminoethyl methyl phosphono-thiolate (a nerve agent)

Introduction

They shelled her with big guns. They gassed her. They bombed her. They torpedoed her. They strafed her. They mined her. And eventually they sank her. The mighty Chesapeake went down. The Bay died. Another Federal failure.

For all the efforts to clean up Chesapeake Bay, many environmental parameters are getting worse. This book, for the first time, puts much of the blame for the pollution of the Chesapeake Bay, squarely on the federal government. The federal government is also in the best position to take charge of the cleanup and restoration of the Bay. This is due to its deep pockets, as well as the fact that too many states and local governments border the Bay and major tributaries to effectively work together. For example, instead of forcing the federal government to cleanup the munitions in the bay, Maryland wants to blame the Bay's pollution on bird poop washing off your roof and tax the homeowner and charities.

Nevertheless, the federal government has utterly failed to belly up to the bar. Recently, President Barack Obama, to his credit, issued an executive order reprinted in Appendix I. This order created a Federal Leadership Committee to deal with the Bay. He ordered the major relevant federal departments and agencies to draft a strategy for cleaning up the Bay. This "draft strategy" failed abysmally. Except for parking lot runoff, the federal agencies largely ignored all of their contributions to the Bay's problems. Were the draft strategy a stock prospective or real estate advertising brochure, few courts would have had trouble ruling it "fraud in the inducement."

One obvious shortcoming with Obama's Executive Order was its scant language on federal pollution. There are only 130 words in Sections 501 and 502. Most deal with the watershed, which could be misinterpreted to mean that the federal facilities on the Bay itself don't have to do anything. Nothing requires the cleanup of munitions. Finally, it again places its trust in the Environmental Protection Agency (EPA), which over the years has taken the position that it cannot do much enforcement against federal agencies because of an older executive order exempting the military from some pollution laws.

To the contrary, the Executive Order places much responsibility on state and local governments. It goes into great detail on reducing pollution, habitat restoration, and agricultural practices. However, it says nothing about cleaning up the pollution in the Bay itself or in the tributaries. If all additional pollution could be stopped tomorrow, the Bay would still be polluted for decades from the dumpsites and munitions in it.

The Executive Order requiring a Draft Strategy is included in Appendix I. Two dozen Chesapeake Bay scientists and experts, who formed a coalition wrote comments to the draft strategy. The author independently also wrote comments which are woven in this book.

Worse than that, William Matuszeski, who led the EPA's Chesapeake Bay Program from 1991 to 2001, told *The Washington Post* that the program repeatedly released data that exaggerated its success, hoping to influence Congress. "To protect appropriations you were getting, you had to show progress," Matuszeski said. "So I think we had to overstate our progress."[1] The federal government being inept is one thing, lying is another. (See also "Officials: Bay Cleanup Administrators Hid Failure," *The Washington Post*, Sat., Dec. 27, 2008.)

One of the failures in cleaning up the Bay has been the complete focus on assessing the streams and rivers entering the Bay, farm runoff, and overfishing. Nothing has been done to look at the dumpsites in the Bay itself. However important the focus on rivers is, it is incomplete. [When this book was drafted] to the author's knowledge, no large scale sampling of sediments and water in the Bay itself has ever been conducted. A few individuals, including Professor James G. Sanders, have sampled for individual constituents[2] such as arsenic. Sampling for contamination is the first thing

---

1 "Bay cleanup failure covered up, program head admits," *The Washington Post*, posted 12/27/08

2 Constituents is used instead of pollutants or chemicals. It includes naturally occurring elements such as arsenic, lead or phosphorus, which may be a concern

that is done during an environmental cleanup. Not ever doing it for the Chesapeake Bay raises suspicions that they "don't want to know what's there." On Sunday, January 20, 2013, Tim Wheeler wrote in the *Washington Post* that the EPA Chesapeake Bay Program has issued a 184 page report saying that PCBs, mercury, and other toxic chemicals so polluted some areas that the fish tissue revealed the contaminants. The article referred to a handful of hot spots in the bay. Perhaps this will lead to more sampling for munitions constituents.

Another federal failure has been the refusal to enforce the laws against those responsible for point source pollution of the Bay including industry, local communities, and federal government facilities. So far, regional officials have avoided complying with the cleanup requirements of the federal Clean Water Act by promising that they would meet cleanup goals for the Bay and tributaries by 2010.

The goal was intended to avoid the development of a "Total Maximum Daily Load (TMDL)" for the Bay and its tributaries, which would set legally enforceable caps on how much pollution could be discharged. The target was approved by the governors of Maryland, Virginia, and Pennsylvania; the EPA administrator; the District of Columbia mayor; and the Chesapeake Bay Commission in the Chesapeake 2000 agreement.

But, waterkeepers (watchdogs for water pollution) like Ed Merrifield said the Bay would be farther along the path to recovery "if we just enforced the laws that are on the books. Now that the goals included in the Chesapeake 2000 agreement are in jeopardy, the waterkeepers and their lawyers may get their chance. Three waterkeepers in the Bay region have already joined together to sue the EPA to take responsibility for setting and enforcing TMDLs away from the Maryland Department of the Environment."[3]

Indeed the Chesapeake Bay could accurately be renamed as EPA's Folly. In April 2001, the *Bay Journal* stated, "The Chesapeake fails to meet existing water quality standards in both Maryland and Virginia, mainly because of low dissolved oxygen levels in deep parts of the Bay." Like Long Island Sound, the dissolved oxygen

---

when dumped by man in great quantity, as well, primarily, as man-made chemicals such as dioxins or ammonium perchlorate.

3 Faber, S., Watchdogs on the water: Waterkeepers bring new energy to Chesapeake Bay advocacy, *Chesapeake Bay Journal*, May 2006.

levels in those areas were probably low even before settlement, but have been made worse in recent decades by huge nutrient increases. But rather than develop a TMDL, the Bay states were working—with EPA's blessing—to clean up the Chesapeake by 2010. Otherwise, the agency would be bound by a court agreement to require an enforceable TMDL in 2011.

Rather than try to meet state water quality standards, the Chesapeake Bay Program is working to establish new criteria that would more realistically reflect the needs of fish and other aquatic resources. In addition to modifying dissolved oxygen criteria, it is working on new criteria for water clarity standards, which would protect grass beds, and chlorophyll, which would regulate algae production. Once developed, the criteria would be adopted as state water quality standards. Attaining those standards will become the Bay's cleanup goal.

By the end of 2013, the Chesapeake Bay Program will determine—tributary by tributary—the amount of nutrient and sediment reductions needed to achieve the revised standards. After that, all six states in the Bay's 64,000-square-mile watershed will develop strategies to achieve their share of the reductions. Unlike a TMDL, those plans will not be enforceable. And as noted above, this approach ignores the dumpsites in the Bay.

Although the Bay states have adopted some enforceable elements over the years, such as laws that regulate some animal wastes, most nutrient reductions will rely on voluntary measures driven in large part by programs that share the costs with farmers or that provide grants to wastewater treatment plants for upgrades that achieve certain levels of nitrogen reductions.

With potentially huge reductions needed, officials say they will spur more action through cooperation than through regulation. Right now, about 300 million pounds of nitrogen enter the Bay each year. Preliminary estimates indicate that nitrogen contributions may need to be cut to 150 million to 200 million pounds to meet the new standards. "We're looking at big load reductions," said Rich Batiuk, associate director for EPA's Bay Program Office. "We need innovation and opportunities to try new and different things, and people don't do that very well within the straitjacket of a regulatory program."

If the Bay Program's approach works, it would complete a bigger cleanup than Long Island Sound, and in less time. Its' Chesapeake 2000 Agreement called for a clean Bay by 2010—when the Sound would still be four years from its goal. Despite that, some—including the Chesapeake Bay Foundation (CBF), the region's largest environmental group—embrace doing a TMDL now. "The relevant difference," said CBF attorney David Anderson, "is that a TMDL is enforceable."[4]

By 2010 that EPA approach ended in utter failure. It also did not account for munitions as a continuing source of nitrogen in the Bay.

"Secretary of the Navy Ray Mabus spoke at a news conference May 12 regarding the Navy's role in the federal strategy designed to execute President Obama's Executive Order to protect and restore the Chesapeake Bay and its surrounding communities.

"The Department of Defense (DoD) has 68 installations in the Chesapeake Bay watershed. Every military service has a presence, and the Department of the Navy, as the DoD Executive Agent, is responsible for ensuring that they are all in accordance with strict environment and clean water standards.

"'Our efforts are focused on improved treatment of waste water, *reduction of nitrogen, phosphorus* and sediment in stormwater runoff, and preservation and stabilization of shoreline to reduce erosion,' said Mabus."[5] (emphasis supplied).

Apparently Secretary Mabus forgot about the munitions in the Bay and its tributaries. In particular, thousands of nitrogen- and phosphorus-rich munitions as well as tons of chemical warfare material, some of it containing arsenic have been deposited in the Bay. Many of these munitions are releasing their contents through corrosion.

The nutrient level of soil or water is increased from the nitrogen in explosive shells and from phosphorus in incendiary shells. These elements enhance vegetative and algal growth. This can cause algal blooms and oxygen depletion in water. Dumpsites and target areas resemble point source pollution and can contribute to dead zones, where the oxygen level is too low to support fish.

4 Blankenship, K., Bay, Long Island Sound take sharply divergent cleanup paths, *Bay Journal*, April 2001.

5 Lucas, C., SECNAV Discusses Navy's Role in Chesapeake Bay Preservation, www.navy.mil/search/display.asp?story_id=53312

1

The Formation of the Bay and Its Drainage Area

The Chesapeake Bay is a unique estuary, formed in part by an impact with a large bolide [1]. It is smaller, but similar to the formation of the Gulf of Mexico.

Buried hundreds of feet beneath the Chesapeake Bay lies the sixth largest known crater on earth—a crater created by a 2-mile-wide meteorite that slammed into the Atlantic Ocean 35 million years ago [3].

About 6,000 years ago, the ice age ended. Glaciers scoured out some more of the Chesapeake. Then with global warming, ocean depths rose about one foot, creating much of the current footprint of the Bay. Erosion and sedimentation did the rest.

Although the water flushes out of the Bay, much of the contamination stays. Obviously the shape and middle depth of the Bay account for some of this degradation. The Bay has been the victim of tons of toxic material deposited in it for over a century.

To understand the amount of pollution entering the Bay, it helps to see the size of the land mass that drains into it. This is the Chesapeake Bay Watershed. A watershed is basically the land mass that drains into a body of surface water.

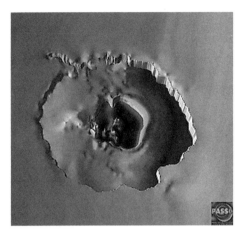

Figure 1.1 Virtual image of the bedrock crater made from core samples.

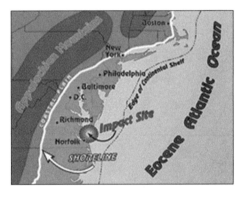

Figure 1.2 Location of the crater [2].

Most high school students have heard of the Continental Divide. It is the ridge along the mountain chains in our western states where the water either flows east into rivers like the Mississippi or west into rivers like the Columbia that run into the Pacific Ocean. There are, however, other divides that separate water flowing into one drainage from water flowing into another.

In the case of the Chesapeake Bay, the divide is actually a circle around the Chesapeake Bay. Inside the circle, the water drains into the Bay. Outside the circle, it drains into either the Atlantic Ocean or west into rivers like the Ohio.

What is often surprising about the Chesapeake Bay drainage area is that it covers all or part of so many states (six) and so many cities and local jurisdictions. In order to educate people, many towns and cities are now putting signs on the curbs or sidewalks near storm drains to tell citizens that this storm drain goes into the Chesapeake Bay. Hence if you changed the oil in your car and plan to dump the used oil into the storm drain, it will wind up in your fish or crabs. Figure 1.3 shows one of the signs used in Washington, DC. A large effort was made to glue one of these on the curb above every storm sewer drain.

The white wavy line on the contour map of the Chesapeake Bay Watershed shown in Figure 1.4 is the dividing line between land that drains into the Bay and that which drains into other bodies of

Figure 1.3 Typical sign used on curbs by storm drains.

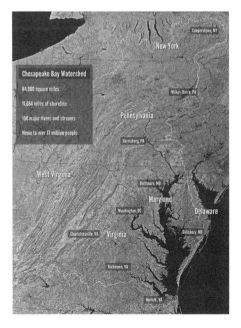

Figure 1.4 Contour map of the Chesapeake Bay Watershed.

water. It basically encircles most of MD, VA, the central part of PA, half of DE, and parts of W.VA and NY.

Seventeen million people live in this area. Major cities include; Baltimore, Washington, DC, Harrisburg, Wilkes-Barre, Cooperstown, Richmond, Charlottesville, and Norfolk. Imagine how many flashlight batteries you discard in a year. You should have three or four smoke detectors in your house, a couple of flashlights, a couple of battery-powered clocks, a radio, and the kids' toys. Let's say you replace just ten batteries a year. That's 170 million batteries discarded in landfills that will eventually leach acid, mercury, or some other material into the Bay, every year!

Remember when the EPA went after boaters? Those sailors actually flush their heads into the Bay! And those awful 2-cycle outboard motors. If we only outlaw those the water will clean up.

Well, what about 17 million toilets flushing on land? Where does all that stuff go? Washington, DC for example has combined storm and sanitary sewer systems. Whenever it rains hard the storm water and the toilet water mix together and run straight into the rivers. Of course that's only half a million toilets. What about your town's municipal sewage treatment system? How good is it?

The engineer that ran the sanitary system for Centerville, MD actually went to jail for falsifying the discharge data. Queen Anne County ran one of their sanitary sewer lines through a little pond that had an outfall directly into the Bay. The sewer line broke discharging raw sewage into the Bay, and it was some time before it became apparent. Fortunately for the county, EPA never knew about it.

Certainly we all could do more to help the Bay. It was not long ago that the author discovered the cheap dishwasher detergent he was using in the dishwasher contained phosphorus. Periodically it built up in the plastic kitchen sink drain line and it had to be snaked out. It happened so frequently, he installed a special clean out port. The phosphorus would form a mound and when removed and exposed to the air it would heat up. Fortunately it collected at a low spot in the line so it was always under water with no chance of setting the house on fire (phosphorus burns when exposed to the air). Now I look at detergent to make sure it doesn't contain phosphorus. Nevertheless, my household contributed its share to pollute the Bay but at least our dishes were not spotted.

Many years ago, farmers were encouraged to leave a 25-foot strip of native vegetation between their fields that abutted the Bay or a creek or river. This not only reduced erosion but absorbed some of the fertilizer, pesticide and herbicide runoff. Try doing that in one of the high end waterfront subdivisions and you will incur the wrath of the local neighborhood association. Fertilizer contains nitrogen and phosphorus, two primary pollutants to the Bay.

Lawn fertilizer is another major problem as much of the fertilizer applied to a dense lawn can run off in a rain storm, eventually entering the Bay. Not only that, but the author is aware of a case where a person got arsenic poisoning from his fertilizer. Many brands contain large amounts of arsenic. The State of Washington actually required sellers to pull a bag of each type of fertilizer off the shelf and test it for arsenic. The results are posted on a website.

References

1. Bolide is a generic term for a large crater-forming projectile where it is unknown if the projectile was sand, ice, or metal.
2. Poag, C.W., The Chesapeake Bolide impact: A new view of coastal plain evolution," USGS, http://marine.er.usgs.gov/fact-sheets/fs49-98/.
3. www.usgs.gov/features/bolide.html.

2

Nutrient Dynamics, Depletion, and Replenishment

2.1 Nutrient Loads and Oxygen Depletion

The nutrient and oxygen dynamics of the Chesapeake Bay have been well described in a book entitled *Oxygen Dynamics in the Chesapeake Bay* [1]; in a 1950–2001 study of hypoxia in the Chesapeake Bay [2]; and in a recent analysis of historical trends and ecological interactions of eutrophication in the Chesapeake Bay [3]. While the focus of many studies has been on the stem of the Bay, there has not been enough attention given to the nutrient dynamics of the Potomac Estuary. A nutrient management study for the Potomac Estuary was completed in 1972 [4], resulting in a phosphorus control program to reduce the hyper-eutrophic water conditions of the Upper Estuary.

For this analysis, we present the nutrient and oxygen dynamics of the Upper Estuary using the Indian Head Station as a control because it has the longest consistent data set and is river-flow neutral, as described in Chapter 6. The Upper Estuary, from its beginning above the District of Columbia to the Indian Head Station, is a freshwater tidal river. The nutrient dynamics are mainly influenced by the Upper Basin river flow, tidal publicly owned treatment works (POTW) discharges, and inputs from the Upper Basin.

Figure 2.1 Two million dead fish in the Bay (the impact of excessive nutrients).

For the dry springs of 1990, 1992, 1995, and 1999 to 2002, the spring Dissolved Inorganic Nitrogen (DIN) pool was half the concentration of a typical river-flow year, during which the spring concentration was about 1 mg/l. Nevertheless, the dissolved oxygen (DO) in the bottom waters went anoxic. In 2002, the surface DIN was not replenished from the Upper Basin. However, the bottom DO still went anoxic for only the month of June. *This suggests that even if the spring DIN pool concentrations were reduced by over 50%, there will still be enough nitrogen recycled to the surface DIN pool to cause the bottom waters of the Lower Estuary to go anoxic during the early summer months.* When the bottom waters do go anoxic, the surface TP in July and August often doubles in concentration to 0.08 to 0.10 mg/l. Most of this increase in the surface TP pool is from the diffusion of phosphorus from the anoxic bottom waters and from the sediments. As the Lower Estuary mixes in September, the TP levels decrease to about 0.04 mg/l. This depletion-replenishment process suggests that more than 50% of the surface TP, which is mostly in the organic form, recycles and resettles to the sediment [5].

Nutrients such as nitrogen and phosphorus can come from fertilizer, sewage disposal, munitions and other sources. This book focuses on munitions because that source can be removed. Also, further addition of munitions into the Bay can be easily stopped.

2.2   Nitrogen and Phosphorus from Munitions

Most of the phosphorus and most of the nitrogen were in the organic form for the Lower Estuary at the Ragged Point Station. Clearly these nutrients are from different sources than elsewhere in the Bay. The source, of course, is the bombs which proliferate around the "targets." Bombs or shells around target areas become dense just like a disposal or dump area.

The importance of inputs, transformations, and transport of nutrients in the Bay, including the Potomac Estuary, has been well documented [6]. These depletion-replenishment mechanisms, inputs, transformations, and transport processes are vital to the workings of the Chesapeake Bay Eutrophication Model [7]. A study of hypoxia in the Chesapeake Bay from 1950 to 2001 suggests that a 40 percent reduction of TN loadings from current levels will be required to eliminate or reduce anoxia in the main stem [8].

Of course much of the nitrogen polluting the Bay comes from the air. I once listened to a lecture where the instructor showed an acorn and a billet of oak firewood and asked the class what was the source of the mass of an oak tree growing from an acorn. I and others wrongly guessed that it was from the water coming through its roots. It is from the nitrogen in the air.

An estimated 20 million artillery rounds and other munitions left over from testing are on the bottom of the Chesapeake Bay and other places [9].

2.3   Munitions Disposal Areas

Some of the most overlooked areas of ordnance disposal requiring remediation are the underwater dumps. Large quantities of explosive and chemical ordnance have been disposed of in this manner. While some of these dumps are located far out to sea, others are in rivers, bays, lakes, and other bodies of water. When these sites are in deep water (i.e. 1,000 fathoms) identification and removal will be difficult, but the pollution to marine life will not be reduced. In the Bay, the main disposal areas are shallow. Even the one disposal area 50 miles from Baltimore is only 100 feet deep at the maximum.

The *U.S. Army Training Manual TM 9-1904*, cited above, states in "Dumping at Sea…General," that the safest and easiest way to destroy unusable ammunition is to dump at sea. The items disposed of in this manner must be of sufficient weight to sink to the ocean floor. Only at establishments located near a deep sea waterway is this method practicable. Port authorities must be consulted prior to taking explosive materials out to sea. In "Transportation," it states that personnel supervising the loading of boats and barges should be familiar with army regulation no. 55–470 (pp. 777–778).

Figure 2.2 Underwater munitions dumpsite.

"The Navy acknowledges that dumping of MEC (Munitions and Explosives of Concern or Constituents) at sea was one method utilized at the time for disposal. However, there was a specific area in the Chesapeake Bay used for dumping by all Naval installations in the area." Citing the late James Dolph, 2010 *Navy Responses to DDOE Comments on Potential Historical Munitions Issues at the Washington Navy Yard*. The author notes more than one such disposal area in the Bay, but if the Navy knows of a major disposal area then munitions should be cleaned up from that area to prevent their toxic chemicals from getting into seafood, and nitrogen and phosphorus from getting into the Bay.

2.4   Chemical Weapons Disposal in the Bay

In cold water, including groundwater, vesicants hydrolyze very slowly. They also only hydrolyze at the surface of the agent. In groundwater or water with low turbulence, the hydrolysis is slow. Also, if the CWM is in a container, when a breach occurs (i.e. it corrodes through) the opening is usually a small area, again restricting hydrolysis. Mustard polymerizes easily and can persist for decades in a lethal form of tar.

Even non-persistent Lewisite, which will hydrolyze rapidly in damp air, can polymerize when disposed of underwater. The absence of sunlight, apparently can retard hydrolysis. Also, Lewisite can degrade into Lewisite oxide, a solid that is still very toxic.

2.5   Total Yearly Contaminant Loads from Federal Facilities Entering the Chesapeake Bay

The 1994 toxic release inventory (TRI) data were the first to reflect releases from federal facilities. The watershed's 25 federal facilities reported releases and transfers of 834,529 pounds of TRI chemicals in 1994. That included: 167,635 pounds from five facilities in the District of Columbia; 205,019 pounds from nine facilities in Maryland, and; 372,597 pounds from seven facilities in Virginia. There were no federal facilities in the Bay watershed portions of West Virginia and Delaware that were required to report. (Really?)

The facilities with the largest TRI releases included: U.S. Navy Norfolk Naval Base, Norfolk, VA – 107,105 pounds; U.S. Navy Norfolk Naval Shipyard, Portsmouth, VA – 100,020 pounds; U.S. Department of Agriculture Beltsville Agricultural Research Center, Beltsville, MD – 79,820 pounds; U.S. Army Letterkenny Army Depot, Chambersburg, PA – 65,107 pounds; NASA Langley Research Center, Hampton, VA – 32,000 pounds.

Nationwide, 191 federal facilities reported releases of more than 9.8 million pounds of TRI chemicals in 1994. Federal facilities were exempt from the law until an executive order issued by President Clinton in August 1993 required them to begin filing reports. In addition, the executive order also directed each federal agency to reduce releases and off-site transfers of toxic chemicals by 50 percent by 1999, using the 1994 numbers as a baseline.

2.6   Sewage Contamination by Military Facilities

Records show three Maryland military bases have spilled about 20 million gallons of sewage into Chesapeake Bay tributaries in 10 years, raising questions about the military's refusal to pay the state's "flush tax," which was designed to clean up the Bay. "Whenever you have sewage spills totaling in the many millions of gallons, that is significant, and this shows (the bases) are definitely a significant source of pollution to the Bay and a threat to public health," said Kim Coble, Maryland executive director of the Chesapeake Bay Foundation. "This clearly speaks to the point that the military has a role to play in Bay cleanup and protection."

Military officials say they've spent more than $11 million to repair problems at the three bases, but that any major upgrades at the Army plants won't happen until decisions are made about bringing in private contractors to run them. The *Sun* reviewed state records showing the bases' compliance with clean water laws after a Maryland Public Information Act request. The Department of Defense has been saying since January that its agencies won't pay. Navy lawyers, leading the fight on behalf of all three branches of the military, say federal agencies are immune from local taxes [10]. Sewage of course is one of the main contaminants reaching the Bay and accounts for some of the nitrogen and phosphorus which spawn the growth of algae. Garden Guru Mike McGrath says correctly that American lawn fertilizer is a high explosive. Ammonium nitrate is the same ingredient that was once used to blow up a federal building. Mike says that industrial fertilizer was never needed, but business owners turned to fertilizer production to keep their munitions factories going after the war [11].

Appendix VIII lists some of the current military facilities in the Bay watershed.

References

1. Kemp, W.M., *et al.*, (2005), Eutrophication of Chesapeake Bay: Historical trends and ecological interactions, *Marine Ecology Progress Series*, Vol. 303.1-29.
2. Smith, D., *et al.*, Eds., (1992), *Oxygen Dynamics in the Chesapeake Bay*, Maryland Sea Grant, College Park, MD, pp 234.
3. Boynton W.R. and Kemp W.M., (2000), Influence of river flow and nutrient loads on selected ecosystem processes: A synthesis of Chesapeake Bay data, *Estuarine Science*, J.E. Hobbie, Ed., Island Press, Washington, DC, pp 269–298.
4. Jaworski, N.A., *et al.*, (1972), Nutrient Management in the Potomac Estuary, Special Symposia, Nutrients and Eutrophication: Limiting-Nutrient Controversy, *ASL&O*, pp 246–273.
5. Downloaded 8-10-1012 from: www.umces.edu/president/Potomac/Print8A.pdf

6. Boynton, W.R., *et al.*, Inputs, transformations, and transport of nitrogen and phosphorus in the Chesapeake Bay and selected tributaries, *Estuaries*, 18 (1B): 285–314, (1995).

7. Cerco, C.F., (2000), Chesapeake Bay eutrophication model, *Estuarine Science*, J.E. Hobbie, Ed., Island Press, Washington, DC, pp 363–404, (2000).

8. Hagy, J.D., *et al.*, Hypoxia in Chesapeake Bay, 1950-2001: Long-term change in relation to nutrient loading and river flow, *Estuaries*, Vol 27, No. 4, pp 634–658, (2004).

9. Group seeks to force EPA to regulate waste munitions at … articles. baltimoresun.com/1994-03-10/...ground-munitions-rena-steinzor

10. Military bases' refusal to pay MD flush tax raises questions, Associated Press, *Bay Journal*, May 2005.

11. Downloaded   08-30-2012   from: homesteadgardens.wordpress.com/2010/03/15/mike-mcgrath... – Cached.

3

Safety Issues with Old Munitions

Although the thrust of this book is the environmental damage done by ordnance and other military toxics in the Bay, the unexploded ordnance in Chesapeake Bay also presents a safety hazard for boaters, watermen, hunters, fishermen, kids, and beachgoers. Experienced sailors are aware of this. "Navigating the Chesapeake Bay can be a challenge, because of shallow water extending a mile or more offshore, and because of major shipping channels and prohibited areas (e.g., unexploded ordnance, sunken ship bombing targets) to be avoided [1]." An unexploded ordnance (UXO) obstruction is noted on navigation aids at the entrance to Chesapeake Bay at 37/05.6 N LAT, 74/49.0 W LONG.

A waterman found an 81 mm mortar shell in his crab pot line off Ragged Point in Dorchester County. The *Baltimore Sun* article, May 10, 2004, states, "Bomb technicians respond to several such findings a year in the bay…."

Baltimore anchorages turned up UXO in dredged material. Due to the recent unsafe handling of dredged UXOs, the Army Corps of Engineers adopted rules for handling of UXO on Hart-Miller

Island. The waterway restriction zone will be in effect from 7 a.m. to 6 p.m. Buoys will be placed to delineate this zone and a Notice to Mariners will be published in local newspapers.

For example, one of those who have researched the munitions issues in the Bay is John Bull. He suggests that only about 80 people have died from old munitions in this country. However, most of the ranges are land based (22 million acres) and most are posted with signage or fenced off. In the case of underwater munitions, these may be encountered by boaters, divers, watermen and kids unaware of the safety threat.

Traditionally commercial fishing causes the most accidents with underwater ordnance. 20 fishermen are injured or killed annually by ordnance in the Baltic and North Seas for example.

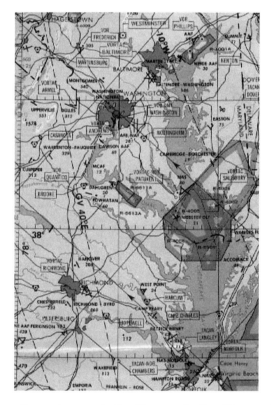

Figure 3.1 Currently used ranges in the Chesapeake Bay Chesapeake Regional Ranges Cooperative: Aberdeen Test Center, Aberdeen Proving Ground, MD; Maryland National Guard; Fort A.P. Hill, Bowling Green, VA; NASA Wallops, Wallops, VA; NAVAIR Pax River, MD; Ft. A.P. Hill; CINCLANTFLT, Norfolk, VA.

3.1   Old Explosives Can Spontaneously Detonate

Hans-Jürgen Weise has spent almost 40 years clearing WWII munitions. "One day such bombs will be so sensitive no one will be able to handle them and we'll have to blow where we find them. We may have to stop as soon as next year," he said in 2007.

In 2010, three Explosive and Ordnance Demolition (EOD) workers were killed trying to defuse a WWII bomb in Germany. They didn't listen.

Explosives like TNT weep an oily exudate. Hypersensitive crystals grow in exudates from old explosives. Earthquake measuring devices regularly detect munitions explosions in the sea, Marc Koch told the 2007 International Conference on Munitions in Berlin.

The British Geological Survey (BGS) issued a recent report in 2005 that: "The BGS seismic database contains 47 underwater explosions in the Beaufort's Dyke area for the period 1992 to 2004." Beaufort's Dyke is an area used for post-WWII munitions disposal.

Some World War I munitions, of which there are many in the Bay and dumped along the Atlantic coast, have picric acid as an ingredient in the fuzes. Picric acid will crystallize and become hypersensitive. At the Naval Research Laboratory on the Potomac River, a bottle of crystallized picric acid was discovered in a chemical storage locker. The chemists at this facility, some of the best in the world, opted to bring in a robot and drill a hole in the bottle so it could be neutralized rather than try and move it.

Figure 3.2 Hans-Jürgen Weise with some of the large bombs he has dug up.

Lead azide, a common fuze material can form a hypersensitive substance known as copper azide if it gets wet and there is copper in the fuze body. Most WWI and some WWII fuze bodies were made of brass, which contains copper. It is unknown whether this process played a role in the Plum Tree Island explosion described in Figure 3.3 or not.

Even without the formation of a hypersensitive compound, fuzes in bombs that were dropped or in shells that were fired are "armed." That is they are set to explode when a certain time is reached (time fuze) or when they hit a target (impact fuze). Almost by definition, they are damaged from the impact. This is a most dangerous situation. Few EOD experts like to move such a fuzed shell.

In fact, there is something called a rocket wrench that is like a pipe vise that is placed on the fuze. There are two blank 50 caliber shells attached to the vise facing opposite directions and fired by electrical detonators. Wires run to a remote location and when voltage is sent to the 50 caliber shells, they burn and the whole vise spins unscrewing the fuze. The shell is then considerably safer, though still dangerous, to move.

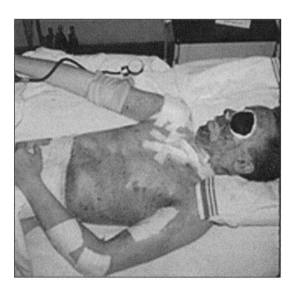

Figure 3.3 Teenager Robert Hastings spent weeks in a hospital after a practice bomb blew up while he explored Plum Tree Island in 1958. He lost an eye and almost died. His mother, Mary, took this photo. A friend of his, Charles Watson, lost a leg in the blast.

3.1.1   Underwater Munitions Can Migrate

Adding to the danger of underwater munitions is the risk that they can migrate or move from their original dump site, drop zone, or target area. In one test, an effort was made to predict the migration paths.

A recent study [2] of shell migration planted 5" shells and 20mm shells off shore at the U.S. Army Corps of Engineers (USACE) Field Research Facility (FRF) at Duck, NC. The first round of measurements was made five days after the original installation. All the 5"/38 surrogates were located and their positions measured. All were buried. The divers estimated the burial depth to be greater than approximately 12 inches because the surrogates were beyond the reach of manual probing with a dive knife.

Six weeks later, "The average movement was 5.1 meters just slightly east of south (parallel to the beach). Each finished cast 5"/38 surrogate weighs 50 lbs and is approximately 5 inches in diameter at the base and 21 inches long." Twenty-four were planted. This is probably close to the weight of a conventional high explosive or gas shell but an armor-piercing shell would be heavier. Nevertheless, the movement was significant in such a short time. There was no indication of a major storm during the six-week period.

During one storm in the lower Chesapeake Bay, several shells rolled up on the beach. Bombs have also rolled up on Kent Island. The author once found a heavy brass anchor winch attached to four feet of prow (heavy oak) cast up on the beach on Assateaque Island after a storm. The winch weighed about 70 pounds and the oak appeared to have been under water for at least ten years and was

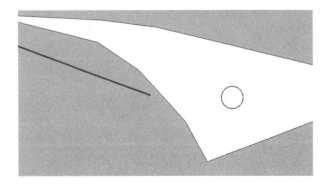

Figure 3.4 Round One measurement for Surrogate #16. The end of the red line shows original position of 5" naval shell placed for migration study. Circle shows location 3 to 4 meters south (parallel to the shore) five days later.

waterlogged. Nevertheless the storm cast it up like a cork. Little wonder that ordnance is often found on beaches after storms.

Migration refers to the movement of ordnance deposited under water or fired on water ranges. The ability of the underwater munitions to move can be important to human contact. We use the term migration here in the broadest sense to include the scattering effect of ordnance thrown overboard due to boat drift and lateral directional movement while sinking because of the shape of the ordnance item and/or currents (described in more detail under the heading "density").

The author has chosen to separate bombing targets, artillery ranges, and mined areas into separate chapters. In reality, many of these areas could have, and probably do have, two or three types of ordnance as the picture in Figure 3.5 taken at a range in Puerto Rico indicates.

Once their skins corrode away, bombs and other thin-skinned ordnance like chemical weapons, will pollute surrounding marine life. Also, they can become more buoyant, migrating easier, especially those filled with nitrocellulose or phosphorus. They can drift into boat paths or onto beaches. Landmines are now often made of plastic to avoid detection, and can float if implanted on a beach or eroded from land during a flood. Some mines for ships are designed to float and can drift if they break away from their moorings.

Figure 3.5 A 500 lb bomb in background; armed projectile in foreground (note rifling grooves); Vieques, Puerto Rico.
Source: Jim Barton

Migration also includes the rolling of ordnance during storm events or in strong currents. Storms frequently cast or roll even large, heavy shells up onto beaches. "Royal Navy bomb disposal experts are being called out daily to detonate unexploded bombs, mines and shells washed up on Scotland's beaches. The Ministry of Defence estimates almost 2,000 potentially lethal explosive devices are washed ashore each year [3]."

The strong winds and heavy rains from the 2004 landfall of Hurricane Jeanne partially exposed an unexploded 10-foot long Tiny Tim rocket in the driveway of a Florida residence. EOD responded and removed the 1940s-era rocket. These rockets were used in training for WWII's D-Day invasion. A few days following the discovery of this rocket, a second unexploded rocket was found along the seawall near where the first rocket was found. In 2004, EOD teams in Florida responded to five explosives and emergency calls after hurricanes [4].

The first Ocean Dumping event of chemical weapons involved the steamer Elinor in January, 1919. The boat was loaded with chemical munitions and drums of liquid agent at the Bush River Depot. It began dumping the drums after leaving the mouth of the Chesapeake Bay. The crew soon learned that some of the drums of mustard floated, and after that they positioned a sharpshooter to shoot the "floaters." (Note: Airspace is left in bombs, shells and drums filled with liquid agent so that the agent will not leak if it expands in hot weather.) This can cause thin-skinned bombs and drums to float if too much air is left.

In 2012, a one ton chemical cylinder washed up on the shore at the southeast side of the Bay bridge from the flooding caused by Hurricane Lee. It is unknown whether this was from Aberdeen or some other chemical facility.

Often ordnance items are pumped in with sand to replen-ish eroded beaches. The U.S. Army Corps of Engineers says that more than 1,100 munitions were discovered on the beaches in Surf City following a beach-replenishment project [5]. Ordnance is also dredged up from river or bay channel bottoms and winds up in dredge spoils. Artificial islands, constructed from dredged spoils, are used for airstrips, housing, and resorts. Ordnance is frequently moved or raised while being caught in fishing seines, crab drags, and oyster or clam dredging or tonging.

The Danforth-style anchor has been an immense improvement for small boats, as its widespread acceptance implies. However, it also has the unfortunate ability to snag ordnance items while weighing anchor.

Figure 3.6 Five-inch shells after salt water disposal.

Figure 3.7 Fragmentation bomb from the Atlantic showing the complete rusting away of the casing.
Source: AMPRO Consultants

A Maryland study stated that a 155-mm shell would not perforate for 69 years in clay soils. The penetration time of the thinnest section for most ordnance was predicted to be < 30 years [6]. 2,4-DNT and TNT was extracted from multiple sediment samples in Halifax Harbor, Canada, indicating that slow leakage was occurring to intact ordnance undisturbed for 50 years [7]. This could be faster in warmer water like the Bay.

Bombs are thin-cased munitions. Planes have limited weight capacity and more bombs can be carried if they have thin skins. Bomb skins corrode much faster than shells.

3.1.2 Density

There are three primary ways that ordnance ends up under water: Dumping (disposal); firing or bombing (in training or combat), and; sinking of war or supply ships. The Bay has no sunken ships with munitions but does have dump or disposal sites and ranges.

Underwater ordnance resulting from combat and that from target practice generally is found in a scattered pattern. Often there is a denser concentration closer to the target. Typically, wide area assessments are done to find the area of greatest concentration and those areas are prioritized.

Ordnance dumped from a moving vessel is, of course, scattered. In deeper water, ordnance dumped from a stationary vessel can also be scattered due to drift as it is sinking. Even in shallow water, the drift of the barge or boat can scatter ordnance. (In fact, it is unwise to anchor a barge or boat used to dump ordnance, since an item could become tangled in the anchor or rode and detonate upon the anchor reaching the hull.

3.1.3 Wide Area Assessments [8]

A variety of metal detectors can be used for wide area assessments. Generally, a boat-mounted detector (twin beam magnetometers) or one mounted on an underwater planing sled to prevent snagging or bumping into a UXO item are used. For munitions sunk into silt, a towed array on wheels can be used. In either case, wide lanes are used and a computer program that will give density statistical calculations is required. The advent of detailed sonar allows a wide area assessment.

Wide area assessments can also be conducted for environmental conditions.

3.1.4 Human Death from Underwater UXO Detonations

"In July 1965, such a tragedy took place aboard the fishing vessel *Snoopy*. The *Snoopy* was trawling for scallops off the coast of North Carolina when it caught a large cylinder-shaped item in its net. A

Figure 3.8 This Baltic fisherman appears to have snagged a German torpedo.

witness said he could clearly see a long round object swaying in the net amidships over the *Snoopy*. What happened next is unclear; but an explosion occurred that caused the loss of the *Snoopy* and eight members of the crew [9]."

Was it a torpedo or a rocket?

3.1.5   Human Death or Injury from Chemical Underwater UXO

"Most of the sulfur mustard found in Germany after World War II was dumped into the Baltic Sea. Between 1966 and 2002, fishermen have found around 700 chemical weapons in the Bornholm region, most of which contained sulfur mustard. One of the more frequently dumped weapons was the "Sprühbüchse 37" (SprüBü37, Spray Can 37, 1937 being the year of its fielding with the German Army). These weapons contain sulfur mustard mixed with a thickener, which renders it a tar-like viscosity. When the content of the SprüBü37 comes in contact with water, only the sulfur mustard in the outer layers of the lumps of viscous mustard hydrolyses, leaving amber-colored residues which still contain most of the active sulfur mustard. On mechanically breaking these lumps, e.g. with a fishing net's drag board or with the hands, the enclosed sulfur mustard is still as active as it has been at the time the weapon has been dumped. These lumps, when washed ashore, can be mistaken for amber, which can lead to severe health problems [10]."

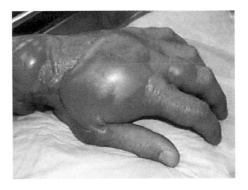

Figure 3.9 Dover Air Force Base EOD tech's hand after blowing up a 75 mm mustard gas shell.

"In 1972, the United States Congress banned the practice of disposing chemical weapons into the ocean. However, 64 million pounds of nerve and mustard agents had already been dumped into the ocean waters off the United States by the U.S. Army. According to a 1998 report created by William Brankowitz, deputy project manager in the U.S. Army Chemical Materials Agency, the Army created at least 26 chemical weapons dump sites in the ocean off at least 11 states on both the west and east coasts. Additionally because of poor records, they currently only know the rough whereabouts of half of them [11]."

Clam and oyster shells are sold as driveway paving material. Ordnance items have been found in scores of driveways in New Jersey, Delaware, and Maryland. One driveway had a 75 mm mustard gas shell. The gas had polymerized after the shell rusted through.

Although this gas shell came from clam dredging off the coast, it could as well have been dredged up with bay oysters. The shell most likely originated at Aberdeen Proving Ground as many were tested on ranges there. At least one and possibly two one-ton cylinders of mustard are known to have been thrown into the Chesapeake Bay.

3.1.6   Human Chronic Illness from Munitions Constituents in Seafood

Even low level toxins from underwater munitions can escalate up the food chain. The large fish, often most desirable for fishermen to catch, can have the most contamination. Even some small fish like sardines used for human consumption can contain high amounts of oil which can concentrate certain toxins. Scottish farm-raised salmon are often fed menhedan, an oily fish caught in the lower Chesapeake Bay. These fish have large amounts of PCBs from industrial pollution and a Naval ghost fleet moored in the James River. Hence the salmon, raised in otherwise clean water off Scotland contain high amounts of PCBs.

Of course, ordnance deposited in fresh water, such as rivers or the Great Lakes, poses an additional threat if the waterbody is used for drinking water. In arid regions, salt water can be desalinated for use as drinking water. It is unknown to what degree if any, ions such as perchlorate or explosive or chemical warfare material are separated out during the desalination process. This is inherently no different from buried or range munitions leaching into drinking water aquifers.

Several common explosive fillers in ordnance are toxic to humans. *The National Institute for Occupational Safety and Health (NIOSH) Pocket Guide to Chemical Hazards* includes warnings on several explosives. These toxic issues are dealt with in subsequent sections.

3.1.7   Real Estate Impacts

Avoiding death or injury from munitions can cause numerous problems for the real estate community and local officials. An example can be found from a planning meeting in New Jersey. "The planners offered three alternatives for locating either offices or residences along the waterfront, depending on market conditions. They also called for preserving a wooded area east of I-664 for an environmental study center.

One panelist noted a potential glitch: The Army Corps of Engineers has not completed a cleanup of a portion of the site that was once an Army munitions depot. Millions have been spent since 1987 removing TNT and other dangerous materials.

"A lot has to be done before this can be pulled off," said Donna Lewis, Planning Director of Mercer County, referring to the remaining cleanup work. "Allowing the situation to persist will result in no development activity when the market is ready."

The panel urged the owners over the next three years to develop a joint-operating agreement, hire an individual or firm to oversee the project's implementation, take steps to preserve the shoreline, begin developing waterfront amenities, and upgrade roads.

"They've laid out a good program for us, and now it's up to us to implement it," city manager Selena Cuffee-Glenn said. "We're excited about moving to the next level." She said discussions between the city and Teaneck Creek Conservancy (TCC) could begin in a few days."

References

1. Dave Shores, "Charter Trip on Chesapeake Bay," May 23–27, 2005.
2. Predicting the mobility and burial of underwater munitions and explosives of concern using the VORTEX Model ESTCP, Project MM-0417, May 2008.
3. Rodrick, V., Sea shells; Deadly harvest of munitions is washed up on Scotland's beaches, 2006 Mail on Sunday; London (UK). ProQuest Information and Learning.
4. Munitions True Stories. Downloaded 02-22-2013 from: articles.orlandosentinel.com/keyword/hurricane-jeanne October 1, 2004,*Vero Beach Press Journal*, SunSentinel.com
5. Weaver, D. WWI ship's log shows it dumped munitions off Surf City, *Atlantic City Press*, Sunday, September 07, 2008.
6. Epstein, *et al.*, 1973.
7. Darrach, M.R., Chutjian, A. and Plett, G.A. (1998), Trace explosives signatures from World War II unexploded undersea ordnance, *Environmental Science and Technology*, 32, 1354-1358.
8. Bucaro, J.A., Houston, B.H., Saniga, M., Nelson, H., Yoder, T., Kraus, L., and L. Carin L., Wide area detection and identification of underwater UXO using structural acoustic sensors, Naval Research Lab, Washington DC, January 2007.
9. *Munitions at Sea: A Guide for Commercial Maritime Industries*, prepared by the Defense Ammunition Center U.S. Army Technical Center for Explosives Safety (USATCES),(918) 420-8919. See also, *A Fisherman's Guide to Explosive Ordnance*, UNC Sea Grant College Publication UNC-SG-81-05, May 1981.
10. Wikipedia.
11. Ibid.

4

Artillery Shells in the Bay

The U.S. military has long chosen the Chesapeake as a venue to practice firing and testing artillery and other ordnance. "While rummaging through the box at the stern of a clam dredge boat I once bought, we found two old artillery projectiles that the boat's previous owners had dredged up. One, scraped clean, bore a brass manufacturer's date of 1898—the Spanish American War…. [1]"

4.1 Bloodsworth Island Range

"One morning, in the early 1970s, my wife, Nancy, was at the helm as we followed John Smith's course out of Hooper Straits. I'd gone below for something. There was a stiff breeze and a sudden concussion shook the boat. I vaulted topsides, sure that we'd blown out a sail, and looked forward to find a Naval vessel almost dead on our bow with smoke drifting to port from her guns as she shelled poor Bloodsworth. She'd fired virtually over our heads with no warning [2]."

The author had a similar experience in 1972 while bringing his houseboat up the Potomac River at Indianhead. He passed a Navy launch with a banner that said "RANGE BOAT." Several sailors

29

appeared to be asleep in the cockpit. Farther up the river, two muffled explosions (estimated to be from a three inch shell) with large water columns occurred about a hundred feet off his port bow. Shortly beyond that, a very angry looking officer at the helm of a similar Navy launch opened the throttle on his diesel engine as he took off to raise hell with the lower boat for allowing the author through. In cutting across my bow, he threw up a five-foot wave which tore the canvas off my rail, forced open my door, and flooded my cabin. Too bad they don't give a Friendly Fire medal.

Bloodsworth Island is a large expanse of marshy land used by the Navy as an artillery range. The Bloodsworth Island Range (BIR) is comprised of four islands (Adam, Bloodsworth, Northeast, and Pone) with a combined land area of 6,013 acres. Bloodsworth Island is the largest at 5,361 acres. A fifth island, Great Cove, was formerly part of the BIR but is now completely submerged. The BIR was acquired by the Navy during World War II (July 1942) and was in continuous use for BIR operations until 1996 [3].Obviously, if they shelled and bombed Great Cove island into nonexistence, that created environmental damage.

It is estimated that over 230,000 naval shells were fired into the area. Ordnance delivered by aircraft included non-explosive training rounds, non-explosive practice bombs, and explosive ordnance up to 500 pounds. In addition, illumination flares, 2.75-inch and 5-inch rockets, and machine guns were employed. (The flares and rockets probably added perchlorate contamination to the area.)

The United States Navy proposes to increase the use of the BIR land and surface water resources for research, development, test, and evaluation (RDT&E) and selected training operations. Probably the reason they are proposing this is that if it is an active range, they don't have to clean up the UXO and other Military Munitions Related Contaminants (MMRCs). This is similar to the Coast Guard trying to make much of the Great Lakes into a "machine gun range" so the military would not have to clean up the bombs, shells, and other ordnance littering the Lakes from prior range and disposal activities.

Naval shells are generally base fused. That means that the nose of the shell, called the ogive, is simply pointed so that it can better penetrate the armor plating on a ship and then explode. By contrast Army shells are generally nose fused and are intended to explode as soon as they strike the ground, tree, or structure, scattering their shrapnel among any enemy troops in the vicinity. Both types of shells from the era when Bloodsworth Island was utilized, generally had impact fuses.

Either shell type is likely to have a high dud ratio when fired into water or marshy ground. However, base-fused shells will have a much higher dud ratio in this circumstance than nose-fused shells. World War I shells had a dud ratio of about 30%. World War II designs had a dud ratio of about 15% when employed as intended.

The Bloodsworth Island Range was used for Research and Development Training and Evaluation operations and incorporating selected training events. Probably the early shells that were fired there were leftover WWI shells. Altogether the dud ratio could be as high as 20–25%. Thus there could be 50,000 live shells buried in the sand and muck.

The Maryland Department of Natural Resources in its 2009 hunting booklet correctly says, "Bloodsworth Island Range is an active military bombing range located in Dorchester County, MD. Warning: Because of the threat of unexploded ordnance hunters must adhere to special restrictions at all times."

The Navy considered allowing resumption of previous range operations that involved nonexplosive ordnance for air-to-ground impact operations on Bloodsworth and Pone Islands; and range operations, compatible with natural resources management procedures at the BIR which involve small boat platforms, amphibious craft, rotary- and fixed-wing aircraft, small arms (training and operational rounds), and ground forces [4].

While nonexplosive ordnance is an improvement, rockets still contain perchlorate, or worse, rocket fuels, and small arms ammo contains lead and antimony. Finally, maintaining an active range allows the military to avoid cleaning up the explosive ordnance and munitions constituents already on the range.

The Navy also says, "…nor would these effects pose disproportionate environmental health or safety risks to children pursuant to Executive Order 13045 [5]."It's difficult to look at the photograph of the teenager Robert Hastings (Figure 3.3) injured exploring Plum Point and believe this statement. Ranges and the ordnance found there constitute an attractive nuisance for children. Teenagers younger than 16 often explore areas in the Bay region by boat, since they don't need a driver's license.

"When she was a youngster on Deal Island, which directly faced the action several miles to the west, Ashley Parkinson told the *Delmarva Daily Times* that she used to sit on the beach and watch the bombs fall. "You could tell which were the bombs and which were the duds [6]."

Figure 4.1 Bloodsworth Island Navy fighter crash site.

Of course it's the duds that pose the safety problems.

4.1.1   Baltimore Anchorages

Recent unsafe handling of dredged UXOs led the Army Corps of Engineers to adopt rules for handling of UXO on Hart-Miller Island. The waterway restriction zone will be in effect from 7 a.m. to 6 p.m. Buoys will be placed to delineate this zone and a "Notice to Mariners" will be published in local newspapers.

4.1.2   Fort Armistead

"Abandoned in 1923 and claimed by the City of Baltimore in 1928. Used as a Navy ammunition dump during World War II and returned to the City in 1947 [7]." A disposal area on the charts exists off Fort Armistead, which further suggests munitions dumping.

4.1.3   Proximity-Fuze Testing

Proximity fuzes contain little metal detectors that cause the anti-aircraft shells to explode when close enough to an airplane to damage it. The United States Navy tested proximity-fuzed ammunition against drone aircraft targets over Chesapeake Bay in August, 1942, from gun batteries aboard the cruiser USS Cleveland (CL-55). The tests were so successful that all target drones were destroyed before testing was complete [8, 9]. Proximity-fuzed munitions are dangerous because most metal detectors (and possibly cell phones) can cause them to detonate.

4.2   Seacoast Artillery

Seacoast Artillery sites were designated by the 1886 Endicott Board. Three sites impacted the Chesapeake Bay: Baltimore, MD; Washington, DC; and Hampton Roads, VA [10]. This expanded to four 1902 Actual sites: Baltimore, MD; Washington, DC; Hampton Roads, VA; and Entrance to Chesapeake Bay at Cape Henry. The 1906 Taft Board also added Entrance to Chesapeake Bay.

WWI shore defenses were under the control of the Coast Artillery. Since the Coast Artillery organization was subsequently merged into other Army and Navy branches, it is sometimes difficult to find records. However, it is likely that guns were fired for practice and that leftover ammunition was dumped when the site was closed. There is a disposal site in the Bay just south of the Baltimore site.

4.2.1   Fort Smallwood (1896–1928)

Fort Smallwood is located in Rock Point, Maryland, at the Patapsco River entrance opposite Fort Howard. Located on a 100-acre tract in Anne Arundel County, Maryland, it was purchased by the Federal Government in 1896. Battery construction began in 1899 and the first battery was completed in 1900. It had two six-inch guns on disappearing carriages and two three-inch guns on pedestal mounts.

Figure 4.2 Battery Hartshorne panorama [11].

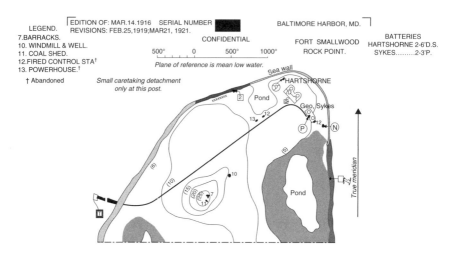

Figure 4.3 The gun emplacements are shown on the point of the land as two little circles inside two structures on the point of land.

4.2.2   Fort Monroe, VA

As many as 23,000 munitions could be scattered throughout Fort Monroe, and 80,000 or so more in the moat, including cannonballs [12]. Anchoring is restricted in that area.

"In 1978, naval ordnance specialists removed the top 2 feet of sediment in the moat and discovered 182 cannonballs, 25,000 rounds of small-arms ammunition and more than 2,000 fuses, according to base officials. A few years ago at nearby Buckroe Beach, a beachcomber with a metal detector found a spent artillery shell. That find

Figure 4.4 Rodman Gun Battery at Fort Monroe during 1864.

Figure 4.5 Aerial view of Fort Monroe.

and others prompted an emergency review by the Army Corps of Engineers. Project workers found about 20 rounds of 45 mm, 75 mm and 76 mm anti-aircraft ammunition. They may have come from a beach-replenishment project in which sand was dredged from former artillery ranges near the Chesapeake Bay [13]."

"For much of the last 200 years at Fort Monroe, cannons and gigantic guns have fired projectiles out over the water—some as big as 1,000 pounds and heavier. Cannonballs and munitions shot from Fort Monroe and Fort Wool could have landed in an area as large as 134,977 acres of the Chesapeake Bay and Hampton Road, according to the Final Historical Records Review for Fort Monroe, published in April 2006 [14]"

4.3   Fort Meade

Fort Meade had an "off-limits" policy for years due to munitions. This policy changed dramatically in 1991, when, as part of the Base Realignment and Closure Act, the Army was getting rid of the weapons testing grounds at Fort Meade just north of the refuge.

Years of military ownership helped to save the land from development. But it had its drawbacks, too. "This was a munitions testing area for many years," Baldacchino, a miliatry spokesman, said. "Before the area was opened to the public, a 'surface sweep' was conducted to make sure no exposed shells remain on the land, although it's possible some could be buried on the site." A surface sweep does not remove UXO which is likely to be beneath the surface in soft ground, such as exists in Fort Meade.

"In some cases, the old military facilities have been capitalized upon by the refuge: In the midst of the vast forest, a former artillery testing range has been surrounded by wildlife viewing sites from which visitors may see waterfowl, shorebirds, raptors, and songbirds in the area's wetlands [15]." The problem is that the contaminants from the UXO are continually leaching into the Bay, not to mention the safety issue.

4.4   Naval Research Laboratory – Chesapeake Bay Detachment

A request for a proposal has been published to "Develop a Programmatic Environmental Assessment to evaluate the potential environmental effects from past, current and potential future operations conducted at NRL-CBD.

Activities to be encompassed by the PEA shall include those conducted on NRL-CBD's land and water ranges… [16]"

The Naval Research Laboratory, Chesapeake Bay Detachment, Maryland, was a technical leader for the laboratory testing and analysis of RP-12 infrared flare to protect C-17 aircraft. Flare chemicals are often quite hazardous to the environment.

4.5   Aberdeen Proving Ground

Recent projects evaluated both the potential increased lethality and range of the conventional 105 mm field artillery ammunition, 155 mm field artillery projectiles, and a shoulder-fired weapon that can be fired from confined spaces and can meet a range of Special Operations Forces missions, including military operations in urban terrain, anti-armor, and direct engagement of targets in protected/covered areas [17].

An estimated 20 million artillery rounds and other munitions are on the bottom of the Chesapeake Bay and other waterways around the proving ground. More of the old rounds are scattered around the installation. Many of the munitions never exploded, posing safety risks, and some are filled with TNT and other chemicals that can be hazardous to people and wildlife [18].

"Aberdeen Proving Ground officials warn that explosives experts will be detonating unexploded ordnance over the next few weeks.

"Spokesman George Mercer says the series of detonations designed to destroy unexploded ordnance at a remote range at the installation will continue until May 15, depending on the weather. Mercer says some noise may be heard off the installation [19]."

References

1. Dr. Kent Mountford , "No matter what shells are fired in oyster wars, the resource always loses," *Chesapeake Bay Journal*, March 2003, Downloaded 02/04/13 from: www.bayjournal.com/article/ no_matter_what_shells_are... - Cached
2. Bloodsworth Island's flora, fauna too often caught in the crossfire, *Chesapeake Bay Journal*, May 2005.
3. Final Environmental Assessment Operations at the Bloodsworth Island Range, Department of Navy. Naval Air Systems Command, February 2006.
4. Final Environmental Assessment Operations at the Bloodsworth Island Range, Department of Navy Naval Air Systems Command, February 2006.
5. Ibid.
6. Downloaded 11-29-12 from: *Bay Journal*, May 2005.
7. fortwiki.com/Fort_Armistead
8. Brennen, J.W. (September 1968), *The Proximity Fuze: Whose Brainchild?*, United States Naval Institute Proceedings.
9. Retrieved 08-01-2011 from: en.wikipedia.org/wiki/Proximity_fuze
10. globalsecurity.org/military/.../coastal-forts-endicott.htm
11. Downloaded 09-05-2012 from: fortwiki.com/Fort_Smallwood - Cached
12. Downloaded 11/16/12 from: www.dailypress.com/news/dp-22171sy0jun03,0,1936860.story?page=2
13. Fort Monroe cleanup seen at $30 million, *The Washington Times*, Saturday, June 18, 2005.
14. Sturdevant, M., What's out there?, August 24, 2008, msturdevant@ dailypress.com FORT MONROE —
15. Blankenship, K., Chesapeake Bay gateways network, *Bay Journal*, July/August 2001.
16. allenvironmentalsciencejobs.com/jobsearch/display/50548274?xp...
17. acq.osd.mil/cto/pubs_files/The_Year_in_Review_FINAL_5-22.pdf
18. Reid, B., Group seeks to force EPA to regulate waste munitions at Aberdeen, elsewhere, *The Baltimore Sun*, 03-10-1994.
19. Downloaded 08-20-2012from: baltimore.cbslocal.com/2011/...ground-to-detonate-ordnance. Copyright 2011 by The Associated Press

5

Bombs in the Bay

In addition to artillery, numerous bombing ranges exist in Chesapeake Bay. The "targets" are located in the middle lower bay. Large structures used as bombing targets can be found at Lat 38-13-04N Long 76-18-51W and LAT 38-12-59N, LLONG 76-18-58W.

Patuxent River Naval Air Test Center had five fixed targets. The Army had a bombing range called "Plum Point" located on Back River. Bodkin Island in Eastern Bay was also a bombing target.

The Chesapeake Bay has figured prominently in the history of military aviation.

While aerial warfare was a dalliance during the 1914–18 conflict, the real use of aircraft as weapons delivery systems began when General William "Billy" Mitchell, Deputy Chief of the Army Air Service, became convinced that bombs could end the unrivaled dominance of warships as combat engines. In July 1921, he sent Martin twin-engine planes out of Langley Field at Hampton, VA, to sink the moored German prize of war, Ostfriesland, off the Chesapeake Capes. Before stunned naval observers, the ship went to the bottom in 25 minutes [1].

Figure 5.1 Eugene Ely Leaving Birmingham at Hampton Roads in the first takeoff from any ship, November 14, 1910.

5.1   Langley AFB

The trawler Bald Eagle II pulled into port with a load of fresh fish and an old metal barrel tucked in a deck corner. This quickly brought the police, the fire department, and a bomb squad from nearby Langley Air Force Base. Sirens wailed. The metal barrel was a World War II-era depth charge. Packing 300 pounds of explosives, it was live and extremely dangerous [2].

Metal detectors found 17,000 anomalies on the base's Raptor course after an old French weapon was uncovered. Almost 140 bombs were dug from a Langley Air Force Base golf course in 2007, an emergency project completed quickly and quietly and revealed only now. The Raptor course might reopen this summer. The neighboring Eagle course might have bombs under it as well, but the Air Force figures that they are too deep to pose a hazard. The potential problem will be monitored [3].

Chemical bombs were tested at Langley that had been developed at the American University Experiment Station.

A pair of high speed low drag aerodynamic bombs shown in Figure 5.2 were found by James Barton and Richard Albright II using a Model Sea Scan Centurion with 600 mega hertz fish (1200 megahertz fish available for smaller ordnance detection).

These are usually in pods of three below a plane so there might well be a third one outside the sonar track. These bombs are not near any targets, but are within the range fan at the Naval Research Laboratory. Since this range is now closed, these bombs together with any artillery shells should be removed.

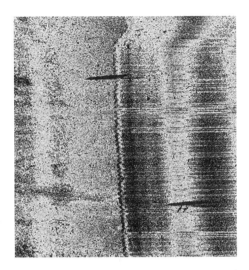

Figure 5.2 Two high speed low drag aerodynamic bombs in the shipping channel found by James Barton and Richard Albright II using sidescan sonar.

Figure 5.3 MK-84 General Purpose Bomb (GPB), 2,000 pound dumb bomb. These bombs have no guidance system and are free falling. This is the type of bomb seen in the sonar image in Figure 5.2.

Figure 5.4 (left) The original Hawaii Mars, a long-range naval bomber, was lost in an accident on Chesapeake Bay a few weeks after it first flew [5]. (right) Is this the plane? No.

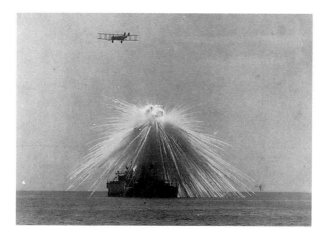

Figure 5.5 A white phosphorus bomb explodes on a mast top, while the former Alabama is used as a target in Chesapeake Bay, September 23, 1921. An Army Martin twin-engine bomber is flying overhead.

The *Orlando Sentinel* reported that on August 16, 1990, "A Navy attack jet crashed Wednesday, killing one crew member and injuring the other. The A-6E Intruder, based at the Patuxent River Naval Air Test Center, crashed near this town on a peninsula in the Chesapeake Bay near the Maryland state line. The cause of the crash was not known, said a Navy spokeswoman [4]." Could this be the source for the two bombs found with sonar (Figure 5.2)?

Figure 5.6 The former USS Alabama is hit by a phosphorus bomb, while serving as a target for U.S. Army bombers in Chesapeake Bay, September 1921.

Figure 5.7 Army bombing tests on the former USS Alabama in Chesapeake Bay, September, 1921, shown from different perspectives.

5.2   Tangier Island

In September 1921, General Mitchell brought the battleship Alabama to the waters off Tangier Island, where two late 19th century warships, Indiana and the dreadnought San Marcos (formerly USS Battleship Texas), had been sunk as gunnery targets around 1911. Mitchell's bombers devastated her superstructure in a midnight attack and then finished her off in the morning with a 2,000 pound bomb that caused the ship to roll over and sink. In 1927, the Alabama was pumped out, towed to Baltimore, and broken up for scrap [6].

Figure 5.8 Wreck of the former USS Alabama after bombing tests conducted in 1921.

Figure 5.9 Martin RB-57 over Chesapeake Bay [7].

"At Tangier Island the three F-105s line up for practice on a 40-year-old rusting hulk laying in the island's marshes. The ship— no one remembers her name—has been hit by practice bombs so many times she is nearly sawed in half. Masuret's first attack is a 'pop up' maneuver where he approaches the target at low altitude, pops up, and then dives on the target. On his first pass a miss-positioned switch results in releasing all four bombs at once, rather than just one. Puffy blue smoke mark the bombs' contact with the water...Parts of the target shipwrecks are still visible off Cod Harbor at Tangier Island, and I used to see Navy jets plunge in to fire rockets into the rubble of their hulls while I was sailing nearby [8]."

Despite the ordnance ranges near Poquoson and Dahlgren, VA, and Indian Head, MD, and at Aberdeen, MD, the military was still looking for more places to test explosive devices. Records show that in 1945, the Island Game Company sold its portion of Bloodsworth to the federal government. By 1948, the whole island was the property of the U.S. Navy [9].

"All morning we heard the sounds of aircraft practicing bombing on targets in the bay, and also heard VHF traffic between the navy and boats passing the target ranges warning them off. But luckily we were far enough west of the target area so that we were not affected. Last fall we were chased away from one. There are a number of them in the bay [10]."

"By early 1944, the situation had changed. Scientists had come up with a means for mating the Norden sight to a combination of radar search scopes. The development provided the team of bombardier, pilot, and radar operator with power it had never known: It could now drop bombs on a target, with great accuracy, *from an altitude of 100 feet, and in total darkness.*

"No effort was spared to cloak the existence of the new device. Training of bomber crews in use of the new system took place only at highly restricted Langley Field, Va. In early 1944, crews trained in B-24s with blacked-out nose compartments. There, the bombardiers learned to operate the LAB system in darkness, even though they were bombing targets in the nearby Chesapeake Bay in broad daylight. Crew members were ordered not to discuss their training with anyone other than fellow flyers [11]."

5.3   Atlantic Test Ranges, Patuxent River, Maryland

The inshore operating area, known as the Chesapeake Test Range, consists of selected targets and airspace covering regions over the Chesapeake Bay, Maryland, Delaware and Virginia. Additional air/sea space is available in the Atlantic Warning Areas, located to the east, and two exclusive-use surface target areas in the Chesapeake Test Range restricted areas of the Delmarva Peninsula

Figure 5.10 Atlantic Test Ranges, Patuxent River, Maryland.

over the Atlantic Ocean. Atlantic Test Ranges (ATR) controls an aerial firing range.

On Friday, November 6, 2009, about 6 p.m., while working to restore Pond No. 3 near gate three on base, a crew scanning the surface waters with a metal detector for debris discovered an unexploded mid-twentieth century five-inch rocket. An ordnance disposal team removed the rocket from the Pond area and moved it to a remote site on base. The rocket was buried and sand-bagged. The team then exploded the ordnance [12].

"Naval Air Station (NAS) Patuxent River reached an important environmental achievement in 1999 when its Environmental Impact Statement (EIS) for flight operations reached a Record of Decision (ROD). Patuxent River is the first Navy flight test range to achieve this milestone. The EIS puts the Station on solid environmental footing and positions it for the future by addressing current and potential operations. As a result of public involvement during the EIS process, the NAS agreed to implement five mitigation measures. All measures relate to noise.... [13]"

The author suggests that much more needs to be done environmentally. Munition constituents and other military pollutants need to be investigated to see whether any toxins have been, or may be, released into the underground drinking water aquifers, or whether they are likely to be ingested by aquatic life in and around Chesapeake Bay and its tributaries.

Chesapeake Bay, MD (off Patuxent) Navy Jet Bomber Crash, Dec 1955

Posted February 3rd, 2011 by Stu Beitler

NAVY PROBES CRASH OF NEW JET BOMBER.

Patuxent, Md. -- (UP) -- Navy aviation experts began an intensive investigation Thursday into the crash of a new Navy Seamaster jet bomber which was considered a potential forerunner of an atomic-powered airplane.

The 600-mile-an-hour plane exploded in air and crashed in flames into Chesapeake Bay Wednesday during an experimental flight.

Figure 5.11 Posting of an article from 1955 [14]. The photo accompanying the article is of a bomber like the one that crashed while landing on the water.

Figure 5.12 Pax River made history with the first flight of the X-47B Unmanned Combat Air System (UCAS).

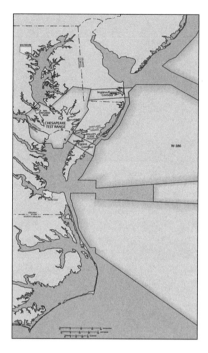

Figure 5.13 Atlantic Test Ranges airspace.

Atlantic Ranges

1. Naval Undersea Warfare Center (NUWC), Newport, R.I.
2. NAVAIR Atlantic Test Ranges, Patuxent River, Md.
3. U.S. Army Aberdeen Test Center, Aberdeen, Md.
4. Joint Interoperability Test Command, Indian Head, Md.
5. NASA Wallops Flight Facility, Wallops, Va.
6. U.S. Army Fort A.P. Hill, Bowling Green, Va.
7. U.S. Fleet Forces Command (N73), Norfolk, Va.
8. Fleet Forces Atlantic Exercise Coordination Center (FFAECC) Fleet Area Control & Surveillance Facility, Virginia Capes (FACSFAC VACAPES), NAS Oceana, Va.
9. NAVSEA Naval Surface Warfare Center (NSWC) Carderock Combatant Craft Division, Little Creek, Va.
10. NAVSEA NSWC Dahlgren Division, Dahlgren, Va.
11. NAVSEA NSWC, Dam Neck, Va.

12. NAVSEA – Surface Combat Systems Center (SCSC), Wallops Island, Va.
13. Joint Forces Command (J84), Suffolk, Va.
14. Army National Guard Fort Pickett, Blackstone, Va.

With more than 150,000 air operations annually, pilots at Patuxent River fly 140 aircraft (40+ type/model/series) over 2,700 square miles of restricted airspace from surface up to 85,000 feet in the Chesapeake Test Range operating areas, which consist of selected targets and airspace covering regions over the Chesapeake Bay, Maryland, Delaware, and Virginia. Additional air and sea space is available in the Atlantic Warning Areas, located east of the Delmarva Peninsula over the Atlantic Ocean. Including these off-shore warning areas, where support is typically provided, expands that area to over 30,000 square miles [15].

5.4   Plum Tree Island

"It only took 50 years, but work is set to begin this month to clear the bombs and rockets that litter Plum Tree Island in Poquoson. Officials with the Army Corps of Engineers' Baltimore District office are overseeing the project, which will locate and remove military ordnance left over from the site's former life as a military bomb-ing range. The work, which will include demolition of unexploded munitions, will run from mid-January into April and resume again in January 2010 for about the same time [16]."

Plum Tree Island is a 3,482-acre barrier island bombing site. During WWII, it was used for practice bombing. Outlines of ships were created on the land. Up to 2,000 pound bombs have been reported to be there. It has also served as a popular camping area, with evidence of bonfires and beer cans. "The island was used by the military from 1917 until 1959 [17]."

Bonfires can detonate UXO. Five loggers were killed in Europe one winter when they built a fire to keep warm over an unexploded shell.

5.4.1   Other Targets

The "targets" are located in the middle lower bay. Large structures used as bombing targets are found at Lat 38-13-04N Long 76-18-51W and LAT 38-12-59N, LLONG 76-18-58W.

Bodkin Island in Eastern Bay was also a bombing target. It has a faded sign saying "U.S. Government Property. No Trespassing." It also has metal track (large, heavy-gauge interlocking metal sheets with holes in them) which are often put on bombing targets in soft wet soil to help the bombs detonate. The *Washington Post*, January 26, 1989, reported that the Army Corps of Engineers sought bombs off Kent Island. The plans were to conduct a sweep along Kent Island's western shore where two World War II bombs were found ashore. The author believes that they were misses from the Bodkin Island Bombing target. Crab Alley, the area north of Bodkin Island, has depths of three to five feet at low tide. Sailboats run aground there frequently. Any bomb that missed its target and failed to detonate could blow some hapless sailor out of the water who struck it with his keel.

5.4.2   Combination Bombing and Artillery Ranges

As noted in the introduction, many of the ranges listed above are used both for bombing and artillery practice. The Vieques Island PR photo (Figure 3.5) shows just such a range, although it is not in the Bay.

"The military has left a perilous legacy in Hampton Roads, from bombs embedded in the shores of the Chesapeake Bay to unexploded artillery shells along prime oyster grounds on the James River.

"As the military has shut bases, bombing ranges and ordnance depots—and as it prepares to depart Fort Monroe in Hampton—it has left behind a landscape peppered with unexploded munitions that can still claim lives.

"And as the region's population has grown with new neighborhoods and business parks, the buffer zones between unexploded bombs and playing children has narrowed.

"Boaters, oystermen, students, poachers—and some golfers—are now at risk. In most cases, the military has known of the lingering danger for decades, even generations. It has done little about it. Some warning signs have been posted. A few studies were done. More are planned.

"Cleanup financing is anemic, and at only two sites in the region have any munitions been dug up—on what's now a college campus/office park in Suffolk and on a golf course at Langley Air Force Base.

"Hampton Roads is a microcosm of a national problem that's pervasive, enduring and mostly unaddressed. Why?

"'I'm not sure from an argumentative standpoint it is defensible,' said Dick Wright, a former head of the Defense Department's Explosives Safety Board, which advises the secretary of defense. 'There are a lot of us who are working in the system and are frustrated.'

"The Army Corps of Engineers – in charge of cleaning up munitions on properties no longer owned by the military – estimates that it faces an $18 billion problem on 2,500 sites across the country. At current financing, it figures that the job will be done in 78 years or so.

"Add in ranges that were used and the munitions dumped on active bases nationwide, and the cleanup cost grows to $70 billion— in an effort that wouldn't be finished for 300 years. That's if no new problems are discovered. Which is quite unlikely.

"A 2002 federal Government Accountability Office audit projected that 40 percent of the country's 9,500 former defense sites were deemed by the Corps to be no problem without adequate research, studies or even an inspection—and often without asking current property owners whether they has found any unexploded munitions.

"In Hampton Roads, a *Daily Press* investigation has found 21 of 152 former defense sites were determined to be no problem with little or no explanation, documentation, or research—and often without a property inspection on file at the Corps' Norfolk headquarters.

"The Corps knows little about a former Navy dive-bombing range in Virginia Beach. It was known as Naval Air Station Creeds when it was used in the 1940s, surrounded by farmland.

"A sign from that era that still hangs on the side of a building reads: 'Warning. Bio chemicals. Keep out. Gas mask eye protection required.'

"The site hasn't been a priority because no one has been blown up there, or exhibited signs of acute poisoning.

"Several large housing developments are under construction next to the airfield [18]."

Another combination range is Mulberry Island, in the James River. It was both an artillery and bombing range in the 1940s.

5.5 Ragged Point

In the early 1960s the lighthouse was strafed by planes on a training mission from the Patuxent Naval Air Station. The keepers were able to wave off the pilots, who had thought the lighthouse vacant.

A waterman found an 81 mm mortar shell in his crab pot line off Ragged Point in Dorchester County according to a *Baltimore Sun* article dated May 10, 2004. The article states, "Bomb technicians respond to several such findings a year in the bay…"

5.6   Hebron Bomber Airport (Intersection of Route 50 & Route 347)

For several years a bomber airbase was established near Hebron, Maryland. It is unknown where these bombers practiced, but it could have been targets such as Bodkin Island, Plum Tree Island, or near Tangier Island. By the 1930s, bombers could carry a sizeable load of bombs.

5.7   Accidental Bombing of Wittman, MD

On one occasion a seafood processing plant was bombed by mistake (not by the bombers at Hebron shown in Figure 5.14). The workers wrote the following poem.

Figure 5.14 A 1932 photo of Keystone bombers and camp of the Army Air Corps 59th Bomb Group. Photo courtesy of the Dundalk-Patapsco Neck Historical Society, from the book *Maryland Aloft*.

THE BOMBARDMENT OF WITTMAN
(POT PIE)

We were working calm and peaceful on the second of July
When the rumors began to spread that bombs are falling in
Pot Pie

It was told to us by our employer since he's just a
jolly guy
We just knew that he was kidding so we took it for a lie.

Wittman is not a town in Europe or any other country
overseas
But, it's a very small town in Maryland – it's our
hometown if you please.

The Jones' were working in their boat house not a murmur
or a sigh
Suddenly, a plane flew over the bombs dropped from
the sky.

One fell near the boat house the other in the field
The Jones' had to hit the dirt for protection and for shield.

What is so surprising and exciting such has never
happened before
Bombs falling in Wittman, Talbot County, Eastern shore.

News reporters, investigators and spectators like you
and me
Will remember July second, 1947
That Wittman, which made headlines should go down in
history.

By the Claw Workers of the
Tilghman Packing Company
Marie Ennells
Conra Copper
Celestine Caldwell
Eunice McNair
Lottie Pinkney

References

1. Mountford, K., Bloodsworth Island's flora, fauna too often caught in the crossfire, *Chesapeake Bay Journal*, May 2005.
2. Bull, J.M.R., Deadliest catch, jbull@dailypress.com, June 7, 2007
3. Bull, J.M.R., Almost 140 bombs handicapped Langley golf course, jbull@dailypress.com, June 6, 2007.
4. Downloaded 11-27-12 from: articles.orlandosentinel.com/1990-08-16/news/9008160893
5. Downloaded 11-26-12 from: www.cargolaw.com/2007nightmare_marlin.html
6. Bloodsworth Island's supra.
7. Downloaded 11/26/12 from: www.mcmahanphoto.com/af366--martinrb-57b-57bomberair...
8. Thuds over tangier, Student Pilot.com
9. Bloodsworth Island's supra.
10. The Voyage of S/V Estelle, Chesapeake Bay Exploration III, Jim Lea 05/15/2007, Solomons, Md.
11. Nitemare's Secret Score, by Jack Samson, April 1990, Vol. 73, No. 4 airforce-magazine.com.
12. Downloaded 08-20-2012from: www.thebaynet.com/news/index.cfm/fa/viewstory/story_ID/15458
13. NAVAIR Public Release #09-153 January 2009.
14. Downloaded 11-26-12 from: www3.gendisasters.com/maryland/18225/chesapeake-bay-md.
15. *Naval Air Station Patuxent River Base Guide*, NAVAIR, Monday, Aug. 4, 2008.
16. Cawley, J., Plum Tree Island is a target once more, jcawley@dailypress.com 247-4635, January 2, 2009.
17. *Bay Journal*, February 2009 Volume 19 - Number 11.
18. Bull, J.M.R., and Heinatz, S., Bombs left behind, Part one in a series, Copyright © 2010, Newport News, Va., *Daily Press*.

6

Mines and Torpedoes in the Bay

One minefield in Chesapeake Bay had 58 mines lost since planting and an additional 59 mines lost during removal. Another Bay minefield had 64 mines lost during planting and an additional 37 mines lost during recovery. The rest of the mines were dismantled and 15,000 pounds of TNT was dumped[1]. Other ordnance disposal areas include Ft. Armistead.

As noted in other sections, ordnance on the bottom of the seafloor creates structures that attract marine life. Whether the life form is a fish or a mussel or an oyster, it will accumulate explosive toxic substances that leach out of the munitions. Mines are no exception. Indeed some mines are hollow. Although the mine shown in Figure 6.1 is in England, it is like some of the mines in Chesapeake Bay. While the Bay does not have lobsters, this photo clearly demonstrates how marine life is attracted to structures. The lobster refused to leave and ultimately the EOD unit that blew the mine up had to sacrifice the lobster. Just as well as any human or other predator who ate him probably would have gotten a large dose of toxins.

Figure 6.1 Lobster living in a hollow mine in England.

"The Bay mouth, about 16 miles wide, was impractical to net and was defended by mine fields, surface patrols, and observers. The fear was plausible. After all, *Deutschland*, the pre-WWII German cargo submarine, came right up to Baltimore and was welcomed. So it was hardly impossible for a clever U-boat skipper to work his way up the Chesapeake and raise serious havoc in Maryland's heartland.

"The large U.S. Naval Amphibious Training Base near Solomons Island, MD, was placed virtually atop a once-tiny fishing village of 300 people, where nearby sand beaches were available to train for mock invasion landings. The site was believed to be entirely out of sight for prying German U-boats [2]."

6.1   The Disappearing Droids of Chesapeake Bay

June 14, 2010: "The U.S. Navy recently conducted a test of its UUVs (Unmanned Underwater Vehicle) in Chesapeake Bay, near Norfolk, Virginia. This test used 13 Remus 100 UUVs to test new software that enables groups of UUVs to quickly search the sea bottom for naval mines. But only nine of the 13 Remus 100 UUVs returned. Four are missing. The navy has warned local boaters to be on the lookout for the lost UUVs, as some of them may simply be floating, dead in the water. This presents a danger to boaters, especially those in small speed boats.

"The Remus 100 is a 37 kg/80 pound vehicle that looks like a small torpedo. They are 1.75 meters/5.4 feet long and 190mm in diameter. Carrying a side scanning sonar, and other sensors, a Remus 100 can stay under water for 22 hours, traveling at a cruising speed of five kilometers an hour (top speed is nearly twice that.) The UUV can operate up to 100 kilometers from its operator, and dive to 100 meters/300 feet. The Remus keeps costs down by using GPS, in addition to inertial guidance. The UUV surfaces every hour or two to get a GPS fix, receive instructions and transmit data, and then goes back to doing what it was programmed to do. It's not uncommon for a Remus to get lost while doing its job, but four at once is a bit odd. The UUV has an emergency transponder, which has not worked in this case.

"Remus 100 was designed mainly for civilian applications (inspecting underwater facilities, pollution monitoring, underwater survey or search). But there are similar military and police applications, like searching for mines, or other terrorist activities. The U.S. Navy uses Remus, as do many other chores. This is in addition to many tasks conceived by the many civilian users. Australia and New Zealand also use Remus 100, and over 200 are in use (about a third of all UUVs). Depending on sensors carried, each Remus costs $250,000-500,000. The U.S. used Remus 100 in Iraq, to search for naval mines.

"There is also a larger version, Remus 600. This is a 240 kg (528 pound) pound vehicle that looks like a small torpedo. It is 3.25 meters (10 feet) long and 320mm in diameter. Carrying a side scanning sonar, and other sensors, a Remus 600 can stay under water for more than 24 hours, traveling at a cruising speed of 5.4 kilometers an hour (top speed is nearly twice that.) The UUV can operate up to 100 kilometers from its operator, and dive to 600 meters (1900 feet) [3]."

6.2   Patuxent Naval Mine Warfare Test Station

This site was used to test mines and torpedoes as the following quotations indicate.

"…Not far away in the Patuxent River, during and after the war, the Navy was developing underwater mine technology to take out potential enemies….[A] sub was reacquired by the Navy and taken to the Patuxent Naval Mine Warfare Test Station. Fitted to submerge and surface by remote control, it was targeted with various underwater explosives, a testing program that according to the

Figure 6.2 Torpedoes were tested at Piney Point, Maryland.

Figure 6.3 U.S. Navy Grumman TBF-1 Avenger dropping a torpedo in late 1942 or early 1943. An Avenger was seen over the Chesapeake per this entry: "In this rare photo (not the above photo)…She is predicted to turn left and land between the Chesapeake Bay… [6]"

old-timers at the Chesapeake Biological Laboratory, killed countless numbers of migrating and resident fish—all for the war effort, of course.

"…[T]he *USS Blenny*, a Balao Class sub of World War II vintage…. was the first of its kind to have a newly strengthened pressure hull made of titanium-manganese alloy steel nearly an inch thick…. The word in nearby Solomons harbor was that she was there as a target… [4]"

1944–1945 Development of Torpedo Mk 34 Mod 1 and Two-speed Mine Mk 24. U.S. Mine Warfare Test Station, Solomons, MD.

It is unknown whether any torpedoes are missing and whether any were live when tested [5].

It is also unknown if any were tested by dropping them from planes and whether any failed to detonate and were lost.

References

1. Box 7 Harbor Defenses archives.
2. Downloaded 09-05-2012 from: www.bayjournal.com/article/old_id/3871 - Cached
3. Downloaded 02-04-2013 from: www.strategypage.com/htmw/htsub/articles/20100614.aspx - Cached
4. Downloaded 09-05-2012 from: www.bayjournal.com/article/old_id/3871 - Cached
5. Retrieved September 8, 2010 from, www.history.navy.mil/museums/keyport/html/part3.htm
6. Downloaded 11-26-12 from: air.blastmagazine.com/tbftbm-avenger - Cached

7

Military Munitions and Explosives Factories

One primary piece of evidence of the vast network of explosives and gunpowder factories impacting the Bay over the centuries is found in the names of roads and places. Maryland, for example, has Ordnance Road (route 710), Gunpowder Falls, and Military Road. By the 1940s hundreds of thousands of people moved to the area to work in factories that made guns and munitions for the war [1].

7.1 Triumph Industries

In 1942 there was a dramatic increase in production at the Elkton fireworks factory which began producing munitions. Triumph employed as many as 11,500 workers during the war years. Most of the workers were young women from West Virginia and other nearby states. Thousands of housing units were built for the workers. Bainbridge also became the Navy's primary training center on the east coast, bringing tens of thousands of sailors and jobs for local residents until it closed in 1976.

Figure 7.1 Company E marching from the Elkton armory in 1941.

"The women who worked at Triumph all emphasized the dangerous nature of the work. Most workers fresh off the bus were given the worst jobs, and those who valued their safety worked hard to get promoted to better positions. Workers regularly were burned or lost fingers because of small explosions. Triumph had its own hospital with a doctor and three nurses on hand at all times. Then in May 1943, two major explosions injured 100 workers and killed 15. One woman recalled seeing a terribly burned man walking toward her, totally disoriented. Despite this harrowing experience, Triumph's workers were expected at work the next morning, ready to 'pass the ammunition' as the popular song at the time said [2]."

Triumph also owned The Carpenter's Point Proof Range (CPPR) now used for residential and marina purposes. The site comprises approximately 11 acres of land located three miles southwest of Charlestown, Cecil County, Maryland, located at the confluence of Northeast Creek and the Chesapeake. From 1942 through 1945, Triumph Explosives Industries (TEI) test-fired military ordnance from a battery located on the southern terminus of Carpenter's Point Road on Carpenter's Point.

Projectiles were fired in one of two directions, either into a target set in a sand bank or down the Chesapeake Bay to a protected range area. Munitions tested were 20-mm, 37-mm, and 40-mm anti-explosive aircraft shells, and 50-calibre machine gun ammunition. Some rounds were shot into a bermed target on the property. Since this was not government owned, it is not a Formerly Used Defense Site and will not be cleaned up by the government [3].

A few years ago, a teacher in California found a 40-mm anti-aircraft shell while hiking on a public trail in an old range. He had it on his desk for several years. One day he was talking with a student and a roach crawled across the desk. He instinctively squashed the roach with the shell. It blew his hand off and also injured the student.

7.2   US Penniman Shell Loading Plant

This munitions plant is located on the York River approximately 35 miles northwest of Norfolk in the heart of the famous Jamestown-Williamsburg-Yorktown Historic Triangle. During World War I, prior to Navy ownership and activity, a portion of the current Navy property was the location of a large powder and shell-loading plant, the duPont de Nemours Company's U.S. Penniman Shell Loading Plant. The Penniman Shell Loading Plant operated under contract to the U.S. government loading shells from 1917-1918. The facility consisted of approximately 3,300 acres and included what is now the Cheatham Annex, the United States Department of the Interior National Park Service (National Colonial Park), and the Virginia Department of Emergency Services fuel farm (no longer active).

"During this time the area included a city of 10,000 people and was named Penniman. The Penniman Shell Loading Plant, which was a large powder- and shell-loading facility operated during World War I. The Penniman facility closed in 1918. By May 1919, less than 100 people remained in the city of Penniman and by 1920 the land had reverted to farmland....Following the end of WWI in 1918, through 1926, the U.S. government operated the Penniman General Ordnance Depot to prepare manufactured ordnance and explosives for long-term storage and shipment to permanent U.S. ordnance depots. At the same time, E.I. duPont de Nemours Engineering Company was decommissioning military ordnance and dismantling the former Shell Loading Plant and TNT plant structures. From 1926 to 1942, the land was in private ownership and was used for farming or left idle....With the outbreak of World War II, the US government construction began on August 27, 1942 at Cheatham [4]."

Hopewell, Virginia, also had been the site of a DuPont munitions factory. In 1973, Allied Chemical's Kepone plant there gained infamy for polluting much of the James River. The author was the first environmentalist to discover this site in 1972.

7.3   Chestertown, MD, Munitions Plant

Sometimes information on military installations can be found from newspaper stories when a disaster happens. Such is the case with the Chestertown, MD, munitions factory. This plant had a serious explosion in 1954. Nine persons are known to have died and at least 50 were injured when a series of horrifying "atomic-like" explosions demolished a 40-acre munitions plant in Chestertown. Nine large buildings were leveled by the explosions. Half the town's 3,000 inhabitants were evacuated from the immediate danger zone while firemen braved death or serious injury to wet down a huge powder storehouse which company officials said contained enough explosive to "blow up the whole countryside." The initial blast occurred in one of the 40 buildings, a long, low structure flanked by two-score others which were built under a dispersal pattern planned against just such a catastrophe as occurred today [5].

As an example of the pollution that a munitions factory can produce, consider a plant in Virginia. With all the current environmental awareness in the military, the Radford Munitions Plant in Virginia still released 12,006,602 pounds of nitrate compounds into the New River in 2010. How much more did these WWII plants release?

References

1. Downloaded 08-30-2012 from: bayville.thinkport.org/resourcelibrary/timeline.aspx - Cached
2. Downloaded 08-27-12 from: cecilobserver.com/?p=734 -
3. Downloaded 11/16/12 from: www.mde.state.md.us/assets/document/Triumph%20Explosives%20Ind%20...
4. Downloaded 08-30-12 from: en.wikipedia.org/wiki/Cheatham_Annex
5. Downloaded 08-30-12 from: www3.gendisasters.com/...munitions-plant-explosion-july-1954 - Cached

8

Contamination from Military Constituents Leading to Environmental and Human Health Concerns

None of the more than 200 chemical contaminants associated with munitions use are currently regulated under the Safe Drinking Water Act. According to the Department of Defense (DOD) there are more than 200 chemicals associated with military munitions, and of these, 20 are of great concern due to their widespread use and potential environmental impact: Trinitrotoluene (TNT); 1,3-Dintrobenzene; Nitrobenzene; 2,4-Dinitrotoluene; 2-Amino-4,6-Dinitrotoluene; 2-Nitrotoluene; 2,6-Dinitrotoluene; 4-Amino-2,6-Dinitrotoluene; 3-Nitrotoluene;Octahydro-1,3,5,7-tetranitro-1,3,5,7-tetrazocine (HMX); 2,4-Diamino-6-nitrotoluene; 4-Nitrotoluene; Hexahydro-1,3,5-trinitro-1,3,5-triazine (RDX); 2,6-Diamino-4-nitrotoluene; Methylnitrite;Perchlorate;1,2,3-Propanetrioltrinitrate(Nitroglycerine); Pentaerythritoltetranitrate (PETN); 1,3,5-Trinitrobenzene, and; N,2,4,6-Tetranitro-N-methylaniline (Tetryl) (White Phosphorus).

8.1   Potential Health Effects of the Munitions Constituents Closely Associated with Military Munitions

Contaminant: Trinitrotoluene (TNT); Potential toxicity/effects: Possible human carcinogen. Targets liver, skin, irritations, cataracts.

Contaminant: Royal Demolition Explosive (RDX); Potential toxicity/effects: Possible human carcinogen, prostate problems, nervous system problems, nausea, and vomiting. Laboratory exposure to animals indicates potential organ damage.

Contaminant: High Melting Explosive (HMX); Potential toxicity/effects: Animal studies suggest potential liver and central nervous system damage.

Contaminant: Perchlorate; Potential toxicity/effects: Exposure causes itching, tearing, and pain; ingestion may cause gastroenteritis with abdominal pain, nausea, vomiting, and diarrhea; systemic effects may follow and may include ringing of ears, dizziness, elevated blood pressure, blurred vision, and tremors. Chronic effects may include metabolic disorders of the thyroid.

Contaminant: White Phosphorus; Potential toxicity/effects: Reproductive effects. Skin burns, irritation of throat and lungs, vomiting, stomach cramps, drowsiness. Liver, heart, or kidney damage. Death [1].

There are three constituents that are on the DOD's list of munitions constituents of greatest concern: 2,4 and 2,6 dinitrotoluene (used to produce explosives and ammunition and known to cause cancer) and nitrobenzene (may be used in defense manufacturing and linked to blood disorders) [2].

Since cells tend to be organ specific, not species specific, similar health consequences to fish, marine mammals, and some amphibians could be expected. Some researchers are questioning whether MSX disease, which has devastated the Bay's oyster population, could have been mutated or exacerbated by pollutants, such as those listed above. Even assuming this is not the case, a more recently identified fish disease producing organism, Pfiesteria piscicida, has been shown, in the famous Neuse River study, to have a link to pollution accounting for its sudden increase in toxicity.

8.2   Perchlorates

As of 2004, EPA reported that 34 states confirmed perchlorate contamination in ground and surface water. Certainly, the Chesapeake Bay has its share.

Rockets and illumination flares, such as those used at Bloodsworth Island, contain perchlorates, a substance of grave concern to infants and women, which is now prevalent in food because of its use by the military since WWI. Most women have half the safe level of perchlorate already in their systems [3]. The study, "Urinary Perchlorate and Thyroid Hormone Levels in Adolescent and Adult Men and Women Living in the United States," involved 2,299 men and women. Other larger studies have since been conducted. Perchlorates damaged neural formation in infants and young children, often leading to permanent brain damge.

Perchlorates also impact fish by causing them to take on the characteristics of both sexes [4]. It is obvious from this study that fish can ingest perchlorate and transmit it to humans when consumed as food.

Several of the nation's fastest-growing areas—including Las Vegas, Texas and Southern California—could face debilitating water shortages because of groundwater contamination by perchlorate, the main ingredient of solid rocket fuel. The chemical, dumped widely during the Cold War at military bases and defense industry sites, has seeped into water supplies in 22 states. The U.S. Environmental Protection Agency and the Department of Defense are embroiled in a bitter dispute over perchlorate's health effects, with the EPA recommending a strict drinking water limit that the Pentagon opposes as too costly. Yet even without a national standard, state regulators and water purveyors are taking no chances: Dozens of perchlorate-tainted wells have been shuttered nationwide, casting a pall on growth plans in several parched areas [5].

Since the upper part of the Bay is largely fresh, it would be nice to have it available as a potential drinking water source as the area develops. The Eastern Shore deep aquifer is largely contaminated with arsenic. The shallow aquifer has pesticides and herbicides.

Perchlorate is what Jim Barton and other scientists call an endocrine disrupter, a chemical that can alter hormonal balances—thyroid hormones, in this case—and thus impede metabolism and brain development, particularly among newborns. On the eastern shore, much of the soil is sandy and a substance like perchlorate can easily percholate down into the drinking water aquifer.

Although primarily a rocket fuel or a pyrotechnic component, perchlorates are used in about 250 different munitions, often in the fuse train. Some specific perchlorate munitions include the following: solid fuel rockets; sea mines; torpedo warheads; smoke-generating compounds; signal flares; parachute flares; star rounds for pistols (illumination rounds); thermite-type incendiaries; tracer rounds; incendiary bombs; fuzes; jet-assisted takeoff (JATO) devices; training simulators [6].

A list of the military chemicals experimented with in 1918 (WWI) is as follows: ammonium perchlorate; perchlor chloracetophenone; perchloromethyl mercaptan; perchloromethyl carbonate; perchloroethylene; perchloromethyl sulphide (sulfide); perchloroethyl mercaptan;

perchloromethylchloroformate; potassium perchlorate; silver perchlorate; and sodium perchlorate.

Some of these compounds were ordered by the military in large quantities in 1918. The EPA's reference to military use starting in 1940 is factually incorrect [7]. Most WWI perchlorate use was confined to signal rockets and flares. However, Germany even had a perchlorate-filled shell in WWI, the 17-cm *minenwerfer*, due to the shortage of some explosives. Amonium perchlorate was also used in hexachloroethane (HC) smoke mixture.

The major use of perchlorate compounds by the military since WWI belies the excuse that they could be from natural sources. EPA is aware of ongoing research into the possible presence of geological deposits of perchlorate other than the desert salt deposits in Chile's Atacama Desert. Likewise, there are some dry lake beds in the southwest that contain perchlorate deposits. However, research results from the Phase 1 study of potential perchlorate sources in the High Plains of Texas (Jackson *et al.* 2003) indicate that no clear source is apparent from the collected data [8]. Additional research proposed for Phase 2 of this study has not been completed. Other research that could provide insight to perchlorate occurrence in the High Plains Region of Texas has neither been published nor made available to the EPA. In every other region of the United States, most notably the State of California, where over 6,000 public water supply wells have been tested and reported, it is evident that anthropogenic sources can be identified for the vast majority of instances in which perchlorate threatens public water supplies (Mayer 2003) [9].

Because perchlorates are so water soluble, they can move readily throughout the body, which is mostly water. It would seem that they could cross the blood brain barrier for instance, affect the sodium potassium pump, or accumulate in other target organs.

The .0007 mg/kg per day reference dose (RfD), set by the National Academy of Science, was primarily based on a 14 day study of male subject uptake of radioactive iodine by the thyroid. That perchlorate compounds damage the thyroid is well known. However, this damage alone should not be used as a starting point for developing a drinking water standard, since there is significant information about other illnesses caused by perchlorates in the medical literature. Aplastic anemia, leucopenia, and agranulocytosis are all caused by potassium perchlorate, and aplastic anemia is a fatal illness. Principle among the other illnesses is the failure of a damaged thyroid to produce enough thyroid hormone, which affects brain development in infants. Infants do not store the thyroid hormone. The thyroid hormone also does not transmit in breast milk. The developing central nervous system in infants is sensitive to small deficits in thyroid hormone levels. This is why the EPA standard has been strongly attacked by the 25 physicians and scientists of the Children's Health Protection Advisory Committee.

The chemistry of perchlorate suggests another potential to damage neurological cells. ClO_4 is a negative ion. It is theoretically possible that perchlorate could interfere with the sodium-potassium pump, the very mechanism that transmits nerve impulses. In a developing infant, any neurological involvement could be significant. Moreover, the theory seems to be born out, because some neurological involvement has been demonstrated in rodent studies. Potassium perchlorate is a major perchlorate compound. Theoretically, ingestion of this compound could add excessive amounts of potassium to a body, upsetting the sodium-potassium balance. Likewise, ingestion of other forms of perchlorate could absorb potassium out of the body by this strong molecular interaction, again upsetting the sodium-potassium balance in the opposite direction.

Indeed if perchlorate interferes with iodine uptake, it could interfere with the uptake of any metal or metalloid. Some metals are used by only certain cells in the body, and then in trace amounts. Environmental medicine is not at the stage where it can measure the trace amounts of metals in certain organs and know whether that level is normal or low. The nanometer is still in development.

The second problem, which ensues in trying to set a drinking water standard, is that the current body burden of the United States population, or a subset being exposed, for example, to a drinking water source, is not known. Little can be done to establish any meaningful science until that is determined, and EPA's setting of a drinking water level is a rush to judgment. While the EPA acknowledges this problem in a one-line caveat, it is lost on the principle responsible parties, which misuse EPA's standards to prevent them from cleaning up lower levels of perchlorate. The EPA knew when it developed its standard that significant amounts of common foods contain high levels of perchlorate.

The Food and Drug Administration (FDA) is currently monitoring 500 foods to see which contain perchlorates and at what level. Perchlorates have been found in some types of lettuce tested in California, and cow's milk where the cows were fed alfalfa irrigated from the Colorado River contains significant perchlorate levels. Because perchlorates are so water soluble, they hyper-accumulate in plants due to plant uptake of water. Apparently they do not evaporate out of the plant leaves with the water.

The most significant study to date was of mother's breast milk. Here 23 mothers were tested randomly across the country. Twenty-two had perchlorate in their milk. Shockingly all but one of the 47 samples had perchlorate. The highest level was 92 ppb. The average was 10.5 ppb, above the reference dose. It is unknown whether the perchlorate was from drinking water, other foods, or a combination of both. Exposing infants to perchlorates even at the average level is disconcerting. Moreover, the study indicates that some current body burdens may already be above the reference dose level. Although the sample size was low, this is the only study to date that indicates current body burdens in the population (Purnendu Dasgupta *et al.*, Texas Tech University) [10].

Thus it is too early to set drinking water standards, even if the reference dose is upheld. Even with respect to iodine, any drinking water standard based on an RfD must take into account the body burden from other foods. The mere qualification in EPA's drinking water level, "assuming that all human perchlorate assimilation comes from drinking water," is disingenuous given the current knowledge about other perchlorate body burden sources from food, cow's milk, and mother's milk.

In May 2002, the munitions constituent perchlorate was found in groundwater within 300 feet of the city of Aberdeen's drinking wells [11].

While perchlorate will be diffused in a body of water the size of the Bay, that does not seem to alleviate the concern. The FDA has conducted numerous testing of foods for perchlorate over the years. One food that is consistently high is shrimp. While we don't have shrimp in the Bay, many of the areas where they are caught are also rich in munitions, such as the Gulf of Mexico, the Carolinas Coast and Southeast Asia.

The FDA studies did not mention where the shrimp came from. The author also does not know if there is some natural biological process that is formulating the perchlorate. Nevertheless, it would be interesting to test oysters and crabs from various areas of the Bay for this highly poisonous substance.

8.3   Lead

Military small arms ammunition (machine gun bullets) often contain lead. Oysters accumulate heavy metals, particularly during July and August, when oxygen levels are lower. Lead can also be accumulated in plants, both aquatic and terrestrial.

Some waterfowl eat plants and can ingest large quantities of lead, making them dangerous for human consumption. Common earthworms can absorb large quantities of lead from soil. Geese often spend much time in fields "grazing" on plants, grain and worms.

Birds also directly ingest lead pellets from shotguns. Whether they pick up the lead pellets thinking they are edible seeds or as gravel for their maws is unknown. The author went pheasant hunting many years ago. He parked in an area used as a shotgun range and had just gotten out of the car when his dog picked up a pheasant trail. Before he could load his gun, the dog grabbed a pheasant by its tail. The author wrung its neck and proudly took it home for his mother to cook. When his mother drew the bird, out came a half cup of lead shotgun pellets. She wisely refused to roast the bird thinking it was ill. Apparently that's why the dog was able to catch it. Hence the author is in favor of non-lead bullets and shot for hunting.

Generally, shotgun (skeet and trap) ranges are private, but often exist on military facilities for recreational purposes. A skeet range at Bolling Air Force Base in Washington, DC, had the range fan overlap the Potomac River. A sediment sample within the range fan showed lead at 775 parts per million (ppm), while the adjacent sample out of the range fan and upstream was only 53 ppm.

8.4   Explosive Contaminants

Nitroglycerin: Two of the more noticeable symptoms are headache and falling blood pressure. Chronic human exposure to it is characterized by methemoglobinemia.

Tritonal: Highly toxic by inhalation and ingestion.

TNT: Exposures can occur by inhalation of the dust, Avoid inhalation and skin contact. through ingestion, and via skin absorption. At sufficiently high and prolonged exposures, more serious blood phenomena appear. These include methemoglobinemia, with consequent cyanosis; hyperplasia of the bone marrow leading to aplastic anemia (because the marrow no longer produces blood cells); and a drastic loss of blood platelets. Petechiae often occur in conjunction with aplastic anemia.

HBX-6 or H-6: Highly toxic by inhalation or ingestion.

RDX: Munitions workers have experienced acute RDX Avoid inhalation or ingestion. intoxication, mainly from inhaling the fine particles; ingestion may have been a contributing factor. The course of acute RDX poisoning appears to follow a general sequence, though some symptoms may be missing in any individual case: restlessness and hyperirritability; headache; weakness; dizziness; severe nausea and vomiting; aggravated and prolonged epileptiform seizures (generalized convulsions) which are often repeated; unconsciousness between or after convulsions; muscle twitching and soreness; stupor, delirium, disorientation and confusion.

Mercury fulminate: Poisoning has symptoms of mercury poisoning [12].

As noted elsewhere in this paper, explosives leach into the environment and are carcinogenic. Generally, the fate and transport pathways for explosives and other munitions constituents under water include: dissolution; adsorption/desorption; photolysis; irreversible binding; microbial transformation; and advection from original location [13]. For example, TNT degradation products include: (TNB/ DNB/ 2,4DNT/ 2,6DNT). The substances found at Aberdeen Proving Ground and the Washington Navy Yard should also be noted.

Explosives cause cancer. They have also been demonstrated to cause cancer in corals and other marine life in Puerto Rico [14]. Cancer rates among nearby humans were significantly higher.

8.4.1   Health Effects of Nitrates

All military and commercial civilian explosives contain nitrogen-based compounds, generally referred to as nitrates.

Nitrates have long been known to affect infants. In infants less than 6 months old, nitrates have long been known to cause "blue baby syndrome," in which blood lacks the ability to carry sufficient oxygen to body cells.

Now nitrates have been linked to bladder cancer. A new study of 22,000 Iowa women found that nitrate in drinking water is associated with an increased risk of bladder cancer.

The researchers found a greater risk for bladder cancer as the nitrate levels in community water supplies increased. Women whose average drinking water nitrate exposure level was greater than 2.46 parts per million of nitrate-nitrogen were 2.83 times more likely to develop bladder cancer than women in the lowest nitrate exposure level of less than 0.36 ppm.

"Our study suggests that nitrate levels much less than that could be a serious health concern," said Peter Weyer, Associate Director of the University of Iowa Center for Health Effects of Environmental Contamination, and one of the study's lead authors. Even low level exposures to nitrate over many years could be problematic in terms of certain types of cancer [15]."

While the Bay is not used for drinking water, many of the rivers and streams entering it are. Also, much of the groundwater used for drinking wells is contaminated from explosive waste from land-based disposals. Finally, it would seem that ingestion of nitrates in clams, oysters, and other seafood would be equally problematic for bladder cancer. In aquatic organisms, the bioaccumulation factor (BAF) is the ratio of the concentration of a contaminant in tissue (mg/kg) to its concentration in water (mg/L).

Many contaminants will also escalate up the food chain. Thus if a minnow eats marine insects that have nitrates absorbed from the water around nearby munitions, the minnow will accumulate a certain level of nitrates. Larger fish that eat these minnows will have a progressive increase in their contaminant level. Assuming all the minnows had the same low level of nitrates, the larger the fish that ate those minnows, the more nitrates it will contain. Since the fish people eat are usually larger, (striped bass that are 24 inches in length for example), they will have a much greater level of contamination than the smaller fish they ate.

In a study of munitions workers at the Radford Army Ammunition Plant in Virginia, ischemic heart disease (IHD) mortality was significantly increased in nitroglycerin subjects under the age of 35 (SRR 5.46). Cerebrovascular mortality was elevated in subjects 55 to 59 years old exposed to DNT (SRR 4.46) [16]. Fortunately the Radford munitions plant does not drain into the Chesapeake Bay, as it released 12,006,602 pounds of nitrate compounds into the New River (part of the Ohio River basin) in 2010. Anyone with a well along the New River is probably drinking contaminated water [17]. However, there have been many munitions plants in the Chesapeake Bay drainage area, and they too probably discharged substantial levels of nitrates when they were operating.

Even low-level toxins from underwater munitions can escalate up the food chain. The large fish, often most desirable for fishermen to catch, can have the most contamination. Even some small fish, like sardines used for human consumption, can contain high amounts of oil which can concentrate certain toxins (i.e. farm-raised salmon are often fed menhedan, an oily fish caught in the lower Chesapeake Bay). These fish have large amounts of PCBs from industrial pollution and a Navy ghost fleet moored in the James River. Hence the salmon, raised in otherwise clean water off Scotland, contain high amounts of PCBs.

Of course, ordnance deposited in fresh water, such as rivers, poses an additional threat if the body of water is used for drinking water. This is inherently no different from buried or range munitions leaching into drinking water aquifers.

Several common explosive fillers of ordnance are toxic to humans. The *National Institute for Occupational Safety and Health (NIOSH) Pocket Guide to Chemical Hazards* includes warnings on several explosives.

TNT or 2,4,6-trinitrotoluene has a NIOSH REL Time Weighted Average (TWA) for skin of 0.5 mg/m^3. TNT attacks the following target organs: eyes, skin, respiratory system, blood, liver, cardiovascular system, central nervous system, and kidneys. Since cells tend to be organ specific, not species specific, one might expect the same damage to marine life as to humans.

RDX or cyclo-1,3,5-trimethylene-2,4,6-trinitramine, Royal Demolition Explosive, or cyclonite has a NIOSH REL TWA 1.5 mg/m^3. RDX attacks the following target organs: eyes, skin, and central nervous system.

8.4.2   Environmental Damage from Leaking Toxins

TNT, RDX, and High Melting Explosive (HMX) are environmental pollutants [18]. Seven nitro-substituted explosives, including TNT and RDX, have been listed as priority pollutants by the U.S. Environmental Protection Agency (EPA) [19]. HMX has been listed by the EPA as a contaminant of concern [20].

However, the biggest share of marine damage comes from munitions constituents leaking into the water. As mentioned, underwater UXO are "structures" which quickly attract a resident population of marine life. Vertebrates and invertebrates, plants and animals, seem to spring up from nowhere. As the munitions leak the resident populations absorb these contaminants.

Like land ranges, some water ranges may be limited to one type of ordnance and therefore only a have few toxins in the water (i.e. a particular explosive breakdown product and a heavy metal from the fuses). Dump sites may have multiple types of ordnance and hence many more contaminants potentially having synergistic or combinative effects.

Some explosives and chemical agents are carcinogens. Even coral can get cancer. Even where the leakage is slight, the contaminants can escalate up the food chain, reaching damaging levels in fish, particularly larger ones especially desirable for human consumption. Chemical agent such as mustard can burn the skin of marine species just like it does the skin of soldiers. Phosgene can damage gills just like it does human lung tissue. Filter feeders like clams can concentrate heavy metals like mercury and lead from the fuse compounds or from the paint on the munitions.

"Mussels, freshwater snails, and other underwater creatures emit a potent greenhouse gas as they feed, according to a study that adds a small aquatic dimension to the impact of wildlife on global warming. The animals, also including worms and insect larvae, emitted nitrous oxide – commonly known as laughing gas – as a by-product of their digestion when nitrate was present in water....Aquatic animals have never (before) been shown to emit this greenhouse gas... [21]" Although the authors only mentioned fertilizers, obviously, nitrogen is a primary ingredient in explosive ordnance. The bigger problem of high levels of nitrous oxide may be its promotion of the growth of algae, and the consequent depletion of oxygen from the water. Low O_2 in the water near munitions dumps may be one of the worst effects from such contamination.

Nitrous oxide production may simply be another issue of underwater munitions needing more scientific research.

8.5   Sampling for Military Contaminants

Military explosives and breakdown products include: tetranitroanaline (TNA); nitrobenzene; 2-nitrotoluene; 3-nitrotoluene; 4-nitrotoluene; 1,3-dinitrobenzene; 2,4-dinitrotoluene; 2,6-dinitrotoluene; 1,3,5-trinitrobenzene; 2,4,6-trinitrotoluene; 2-amino-4,6-dinitrotoluene; 4-amino-2,6-dinitrotoluene; nitroglycerine; nitroguanadine; tetryl; ammonium nitrate; amatol; anilite (nitrobenzol and liquid nitrogen peroxide); picric acid; and trinitrotoluene (TNT).

Other possible explosive breakdown products include: 2,4-dinitrophenol; 4,6-dinitro-2-methylphenol; 3-nitroaniline; 2-nitroaniline; and n-nitrosodi-n-propylamine.

One last rocket fuel bears mentioning since there is continued testing in the Bay. It is NDMA or nitrodisodamethylamine. It is unknown whether any rockets, takeoff assist thrusters, or other munitions use this fuel, but it is harmful in parts per trillion. Whereas, most water contaminant levels are set in parts per billion.

References

1. GAO report number GAO-04-601, entitled "DOD Operational Ranges: More Reliable Cleanup Cost Estimates and a Proactive Approach to Identifying Contamination Are Needed," June 29, 2004.
2. See 40 C.F.R. § 401.15 – Toxic Pollutants.
3. Blount, B.C., Pirkle, J.L., Osterloh, J.D., Valentin-Blasini, L., and Caldwell, K.L., Urinary perchlorate and thyroid hormone levels in adolescent and adult men and women living in the United States, doi:10.1289/ehp.9466 (available at http://dx.doi.org/) Online 5 October 2006.
4. Bernhardt, R.R., von Hippel, F.A., and Cresko, W.A., Perchlorate induces hermaphroditism in threespine sticklebacks, *Environmental Toxicology and Chemistry*: No. 25, pp. 2087–2096.
5. Waldman, P., Spreading perchlorate woes trouble property developers: Contamination from chemical dumped during cold war hinders growth plans, *Wall Street Journal*, 27 December 2002
6. DoD Perchlorate Sources, www.ert2.org/perchlorate/printfriendly.aspx -

7. See *Bancroft's History of the Chemical Warfare Service in theUnited States* 1919.
8. Downloaded 02-22-2013 from: Yosemite.epa.gov/r10/CLEANUP. NSF/PH/Arkema+Technical+Documents/... PDF file
9. Downloaded 02-22-2013 from: www.epa.gov/region9/toxic/perchlorate/MayerPerchlorateDecember04a.ppt • PPT file
10. Downloaded 02-22-2013 from: www.epa.gov/region9/toxic/perchlorate/MayerPerchlorateDecember04a.ppt • PPT file
11. Downloaded 11/16/12 from: www.docstoc.com/docs/82039368/ MUNITIONS
12. MILITARY EXPLOSIVES TM 9-1300-214, 20 Sep 84 Toxicity of Explosives Chapter 12
13. Cullison, G., and Turlington, C., Overview: Environmental effects of underwater unexploded ordnance (UXO) & munitions constituents (MC), Naval Facilities Engineering Command (NAVFAC).
14. Barton and Porter, Cancer-causing toxins linked to unexploded munitions in oceans, www.sciencedaily.com/releases/2009/02/090218091930.htm -
15. Downloaded 08-30-2012 from: www.eurekalert.org/pub_ releases/2001-04/UoI-Nidw-1504101.php - Cached. See also Weyer, P., *et al.*, *Bay Journal* July/August 2001.
16. Stayner, L.T., Dannenberg, A.L., Thun, M., Reeve ,G., Bloom, T.F., Boeniger, M., and Halperin W., Cardiovascular mortality among munitions workers exposed to nitroglycerin and dinitrotoluene, Scand. J. Work Environ. Health, 1992 Feb;18(1):34–43.
17. Downloaded 08-17-2012 from: en.wikipedia.org/wiki/RFAAP –
18. Van Aken, B., Yoon, J.M., and Schnoor, J.L., Biodegradation of nitro-substituted explosives 2,4,6-trinitrotoluene, hexahydro-1,3,5-trinitro-1,3,5-triazine, and octahydro-1,3,5,7-tetranitro-1,3,5-tetrazocine by a phytosymbiotic Methylobacterium sp. associated with poplar tissues (Populus deltoides × nigra DN34), *Appl. Environ. Microbiol.* 2004 January; 70(1): 508–517. doi: 10.1128/AEM.70.1.508-517.2004.PMCID: PMC321275.
19. Keith, L.H., and Telliard, W.A., Priority pollutants: A perspective view. Environ. Sci. Technol. 13:416-423, 1979.
20. Talmage, S.S., Opresko, D.M., Maxwell, C.J., Welsh, C.J., Cretella, F.M., Reno, P.H., and Daniel, F.B., Nitroaromatic munitions compounds: Environmental effects and screening values, Rev. Environ. Contam. Toxicol. 161:1–156, 1999.
21. Stief, P., lead author of the study, Denmark University of Aarhus and the Max Planck Institute for Marine Microbiology in Germany, in *US Journal Proceedings of the National Academy of Sciences.*

9

Chemical Weapons Sites on Chesapeake Bay or in the Watershed

9.1 Aberdeen Proving Ground

"Colonel Ruggles' search for new testing facilities for the U.S. Army took him to the Chesapeake Bay area. He first considered Kent Island, on the Maryland eastern shore, but encountered so much opposition from the inhabitants of the island, that he quickly abandoned the idea. Influenced by a friend, a Major Edward V. Stockham who lived in Perryman, Colonel Ruggles then shifted his attention to an area along the western shore of the Chesapeake Bay near the town of Aberdeen.

"The United States Government took formal possession of the land at Aberdeen on 20 October 1917 and immediately began building testing facilities. The new proving ground at Aberdeen was to be used for proof-testing field artillery weapons, ammunition, trench mortars, air defense guns, and railway artillery. The mission of the proving ground was later expanded to include the operation of an Ordnance training school and the developmental testing of small arms.

"[T]he peacetime mission of the Aberdeen Proving Ground emphasized research and development of munitions. Much of the work done during this period by the military and civilian personnel was in the area of the developmental testing of powders, projectiles, bomb testing, and the study of interior and exterior ballistics.

"During the war, personnel grew to a peak strength of 27,185 military and 5,479 civilians as all fields of research, development, and training expanded and facilities were increased to meet the heavy workload of wartime.

"When the war ended in 1945, the Aberdeen Proving Ground reverted to its peacetime role of research and development. But the Korean conflict of 1950 reactivated many of its wartime activities. Testing of materiel continued as did construction of facilities. The Ordnance Replacement Training Center which had been closed on 14 February 1947 was reactivated on 7 September 1950. Because of the heavy Ordnance training responsibility, the Ordnance Training Command was established at Aberdeen on 13 October 1950 and was assigned responsibility for training all Ordnance troop units. The Ordnance School and the newly activated Replacement Training Center were both made subordinate to the Ordnance Training Command [1]."

"Spread out along 20 miles of Chesapeake Bay, Aberdeen Proving Ground is home to a diverse array of weapons development and testing programs. The installation covers 72,516 acres, ranging from heavily industrialized areas (the base has over 2,000 buildings) to remote testing ranges on peninsulas, bays, and tidal areas. The Edgewood area of the Proving Ground has been the nation's primary chemical and biological weapons development location since World War I, and is now littered with contamination and unexploded chemical weapons [2]."

Many unexploded ordnance items were cleaned up from the ranges by the Civilian Conservation Corps and buried near the low cliffs bordering the Bay and creeks at Edgewood arsenal. Among the horrors recently tumbling out of the cliffs as they erode were jars full of mercury. Instead of "Mad Hatter's Disease," we could change the name to something more contemporary like "Mad Waterman's Disease."

Partly because of the 1988–1989 trial and conviction of three senior Chemical Research, Development, and Engineering Center employees on charges of not complying with federal environmental laws, environmental awareness has become keener at the Proving Ground. Millions of dollars annually go into cleaning up, restoring, and preserving the natural beauty of the Aberdeen Proving Ground. However, the tremendous size of the facility and adjacent water ranges and underwater disposal sites has created an environmental problem on a scale and complexity beyond the current capabilities of the Federal Government.

Just answering the obvious questions is not yet possible: Have the groundwater contaminants harmed area residents? Have the underwater contaminants harmed or contaminated marine life, and more importantly, seafood? How do we sample for the known contaminants?

At Spring Valley, a large worldwide environmental remediation company contacted five of the best labs in the country and presented a list of 192 chemical agents and precursor compounds known to have been present. The labs combined could only test for about 140 items. Of those, about 40 could be detected only by using tests for related sister compounds, assuming that non-detects for one meant non-detects for the group. Since the Aberdeen list would encompass all of these plus post-WWII developed chemicals, one can see the daunting task at hand.

Edgewood arsenal, now generally called Aberdeen Proving Ground, was the world's largest chemical weapons manufacturing and test site during WWI.

Figure 9.1 Aberdeen Proving Ground 16-inch naval gun.

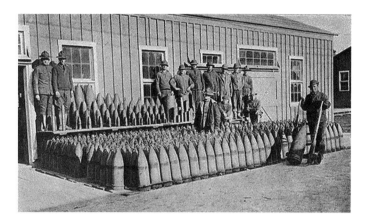

Figure 9.2 This undated U.S. Army handout photo shows a stockpile of high explosive shells (16-inch?) at Aberdeen Proving Ground. Some of these were fired into the Bay.
Source: Historical APG (U.S. Army handout photo)

Figure 9.3 A 16-inch coastal defense gun is fired into the Bay at Aberdeen Proving Ground, 1939.

9.1.1   Training Ranges

- Ballistics Range
- Black Point
- 9600 Impact Range
- Cod Creek/NBF
- Abby Field
- Phillips Army Airfield

Figure 9.4 Antiaircraft guns firing into Bay from Aberdeen Proving Ground c. 1938.

Figure 9.5 Photo taken on October 12, 1955, from the control tower at Phillips Field, Aberdeen Proving Ground.
Source: Photo salvaged by Ross B. Yingst

- CQB Range
- Carroll Island
- Bush River
- Chesapeake Bay

9.1.2   General Ordnance Expended

The Aberdeen area of Aberdeen Proving Ground (APG) was established in 1917 as the ordnance proving ground. Testing of ammunition began in January of 1918. Large segments of the open water surrounding the Aberdeen area have been used as ordnance impact areas since 1917. There are an estimated four million unexploded and sixteen million inert projectiles of all calibers in the restricted waters off APG.

The White Phosphorus Underwater Munitions Burial Area is adjacent to and offshore the main front land range area, which has been active since 1917. An estimated one million rounds of all calibers up to 16 inches have been fired at this range.

The types of rounds fired include high explosives, antipersonnel, armor defeating, incendiary, smoke, and illuminating.

Small Arms

- 5.56 & 7.62mm
- 20 & 25mm
- 50cal
- 30mm
- 40mm
- 105mm
- BDU-33 Training Bombs
- 2.75" Rockets
- Various Pyrotechnics

9.1.3   Specific Contaminants

The list below only includes contaminants identified as contaminants of concern (COCs) for this site. COCs are the site-specific chemical substances that the health assessor selects for further evaluation of potential health effects. Identifying contaminants of concern is a process that requires the assessor to examine contaminant concentrations at the site, the quality of environmental sampling data, and the potential for human exposure.

Media Contaminant Group

Groundwater 1,1,1,2-TETRACHLOROETHANE VOC
Soil 1,1,2,2-TETRABROMOETHANE VOC
Groundwater 1,1,2,2-TETRACHLOROETHANE VOC
Groundwater 1,1,2-TRICHLOROETHANE VOC
Groundwater 1,1-DICHLOROETHENE VOC
Groundwater, Surface Water 1,1-DICHLOROETHYLENE VOC

Groundwater 1,2,4-TRICHLOROBENZENE Base Neutral Acids

Groundwater 1,2-DICHLOROBENZENE VOC

Groundwater, Surface Water 1,2-DICHLOROETHANE VOC

Groundwater 1,2-DICHLOROETHENE VOC

Groundwater, Surface Water 1,2-TRANS-DICHLOROETHYLENE VOC

Groundwater 1,4-DICHLOROBENZENE Base Neutral Acids

Soil 2-HEXANONE VOC

Sediment 2-METHYLNAPHTHALENE PAH

Sediment 4,4-DDE Pesticides

Sediment, Soil 4,4-DDT Pesticides

Groundwater ACETONE VOC

Groundwater ALUMINUM (FUME OR DUST) Metals

Groundwater, Sediment, Soil, Surface Water ANTIMONY Metals

Soil AROCLOR 1248 PCBs

Groundwater, Sediment, Soil, Surface Water ARSENIC Metals

Groundwater BARIUM Metals

Groundwater BENZENE VOC

Sediment, Soil BENZO[A]PYRENE PAH

Groundwater, Sediment, Soil BERYLLIUM Metals

Groundwater BORON OXIDE Inorganics

Groundwater, Surface Water CADMIUM Metals

Groundwater CALCIUM Metals

Soil CALCIUM CARBONATE Inorganics

Groundwater CARBON DISULFIDE VOC

Groundwater CARBON TETRACHLORIDE VOC

Sediment CHLORDANE Pesticides

Groundwater CHLOROBENZENE VOC

Groundwater CHLOROFORM VOC

Groundwater CHROMIUM Metals

Groundwater CIS-1,2-DICHLOROETHENE VOC

Groundwater COBALT AND COMPOUNDS Inorganics

Groundwater, Sediment, Soil, Surface Water COPPER Metals

Groundwater CYANIDE Inorganics

Groundwater ETHYLBENZENE VOC

Soil HEXACHLOROBENZENE Base Neutral Acids

Groundwater HEXACHLOROBUTADIENE Base Neutral Acids

Groundwater, Soil HEXACHLOROETHANE VOC
Solid Waste INORGANICS Inorganics
Groundwater, Sediment, Soil, Surface Water IRON Metals
Groundwater, Sediment, Soil, Surface Water LEAD Metals
Soil LEWISITE Base Neutral Acids
Groundwater, Sediment MAGNESIUM Metals
Groundwater, Surface Water MANGANESE Metals
Groundwater MERCURY Metals
Groundwater, Surface Water METHYLENE CHLORIDE VOC
Soil MUSTARD GAS Organics
Groundwater NICKEL Metals
Groundwater NITRATE Inorganics
Solid Waste NOT PROVIDED Not Provided
Soil OIL & GREASE Oil & Grease
Solid Waste PCBs PCBs
Sediment PHENANTHRENE PAH
Soil PHOSGENE Pesticides
Soil PHOSPHORUS (YELLOW OR WHITE) Inorganics
Groundwater POTASSIUM Metals
Groundwater, Surface Water SELENIUM Metals
Groundwater SILVER Metals
Groundwater SODIUM Metals
Groundwater TETRACHLOROETHENE VOC
Groundwater TETRACHLOROETHYLENE VOC
Groundwater THALLIUM Metals
Groundwater TOLUENE VOC
Groundwater TRANS-1,2-DICHLOROETHENE VOC
Groundwater TRICHLOROETHENE VOC
Groundwater, Surface Water TRICHLOROETHYLENE VOC
Groundwater VANADIUM (FUME OR DUST) Metals
Groundwater, Surface Water VINYL CHLORIDE VOC
Solid Waste VOC VOC
Groundwater XYLENES VOC
Groundwater, Soil, Surface Water ZINC Metals

9.1.4 Carroll Island Study Area

Carroll Island is in the Edgewood Area of APG in southeastern
Baltimore County. The 855-acre island is between Saltpeter and
Seneca Creeks, which connect on the west side to separate the

island from the mainland. The Gunpowder River is to the east, and the Chesapeake Bay is to the southwest. The island is a flat, low-lying area; inhabited by wildlife and covered with forest, open fields and marsh.

9.1.4.1   Background

The U.S. Army acquired Carroll Island in 1918 and leased it as farmland until the early 1940s. The Army used Carroll Island for open-air testing of chemical agents from approximately 1950 to the early 1970s. Tests were conducted only on the eastern half of the island. The Army tested white phosphorus (a screening smoke), nerve, blister, vomiting, tear, and incapacitating munitions at Carroll Island.

Most of the testing of lethal agent-filled chemical munitions involved static functioning, firing downward from towers, and controlled firing short distances into objects such as tanks. During these tests, munitions were fired one at a time. No documentation of ballistic firing (multiple rounds) of lethal agent-filled munitions has been found for the post-WWII period.

The test sites included several test grids, a wind tunnel, spray grids, and small buildings. Carroll Point and the portion of the island north of Lower Island Point were impact areas. The water areas east and southeast of Carroll Island were also impact areas.

Only minimal information is available on the types of rounds used during tests in these impact areas, but it is not likely that lethal agent-filled rounds were tested. The impact areas were primarily for white phosphorus rounds.

Other chemicals such as decontaminating agents, fuel oils, insecticides, and herbicides were used at Carroll Island.

The Army used burn pits and small dump areas on the island for disposing of the testing wastes. Non-hazardous solid wastes were disposed of in the Bengies Point Road. Potentially hazardous solid wastes were disposed of in the Lower Island disposal site. Empty containers, cans, and gas mask filter canisters were found at small sites throughout the island. APG has no record that the island was used for bulk disposal of chemical material.

Carroll Island is not open to the public and fencing limits public access. Warning signs are posted along the shoreline to deter fisherman and others from entering the site by water. The site also is subject to random patrols by the military police and other security forces.

9.1.4.2   Findings to Date

Aberdeen Proving Ground's remedial investigation found no chemical substances in ground water, soil, sediment or surface water above U.S. Environmental Protection Agency Region III's risk-based levels except metals. It is believed that the metals are naturally occurring. APG identified 13 suspect disposal areas requiring further investigation and remediation.

The U.S. Geological Survey's studies found the groundwater generally flows away from off-post wells and discharges to surface water. As an extra safeguard, APG worked with the Baltimore County Department of Environmental Protection and sampled private wells closest to the Proving Ground. The laboratories' analysis found no APG-related contamination.

9.1.4.3   Remedial Actions

The Army and the U.S. Environmental Protection Agency have signed two Records of Decision for the remediation of Carroll Island.

As a result of the Focused Feasibility Study conducted to address the contamination associated with disposal on Carroll Island, APG signed a Record of Decision in 1996 calling for the 13 suspected disposal areas to be hand excavated. The 13 suspected disposal areas (including the Bengies Point Road and the Lower Island disposal pits) were excavated and the contents removed from October 1997 through May 2000.

An August 2001 Record of Decision addressed chemical warfare material and all other hazardous substances which may still remain at Carroll Island. APG is designing shoreline stabilization structures to prevent further erosion and the movement of potentially dangerous materials from the island. Under the Record of Decision the primary long-term use of the site will be for a limited-access natural resource management area, and the secondary use will be for military activities.

Approximately three acres of wetlands will be created on Carroll Island in 2002 to replace the wetlands affected by the construction of the Chemical Demilitarization Facility at the Bush River Area.

As this is being written, the news services are reporting daily about the devastation occurring to the marshes in the Gulf of Mexico as a result of the oil spill. The point is often made that these marsh areas are the breeding ground for oysters, shrimp, crabs, crawfish, and fish. Federal, state, and local government officials in the Gulf

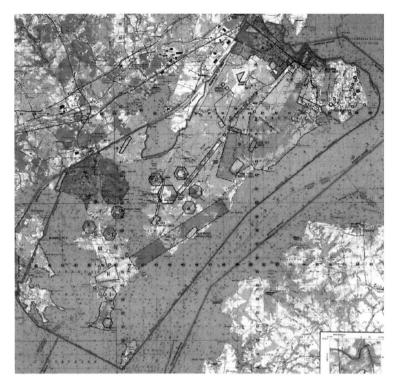

Figure 9.6 Attributes: Open Air Ranges w/Modular Instrumentation Suites; Traditional Laboratories w/Advanced Tools; Controlled Airspace; Controlled Water Area; Domestic & Foreign Land/Sea-based Targets & Threats; Isolated/ Secure/Hardened Surface & Sub-surface Opportunities; Temperate Zone; >52K Ground Acres; Water Depths 2-14′; Up to 150′ in Pond; 103 Miles of Shoreline with 60 Miles Adjacent to Live Fire Ranges; C5 Airfield w/Drop Zones Real-Time MET [3].

are constantly stressing that the fishing industry will be wiped out for 20 years as a result of this marsh destruction. Many of the areas shown in Figure 9.6 are also marsh areas that serve as the same type of breeding area (except for shrimp). Does it really matter whether marine breeding areas are destroyed by an oil spill or live fire and the resultant toxins? Where are the federal, state, and local officials complaints for the Chesapeake marshes?

9.1.5 White Phosphorus

The White Phosphorus Underwater Munitions Burial Area (WPUMBA) is located offshore of the Aberdeen area of APG, Maryland, on the western side of the upper Chesapeake Bay. The area is situated in shallow waters just beyond the mouth of Mosquito Creek, between Black Point and Gull Island (see Figure 9.6). Spesutie Narrows and Spesutie Island lie to the north and northeast, respectively. The open water area of APG totals approximately 37,000 acres of which 15 acres of open water comprise the supposed WPUMBA.

Based on interviews of former employees who worked on the post following World War I, an unknown amount of World War I white phosphorus munitions (ordnance) were supposedly buried in the Chesapeake Bay in the vicinity of Black Point during the period from 1922 to 1925. The ordnance reportedly consisted of United States, British, and French land mines, grenades, and artillery shells. According to the interviews, bulk phosphorus may also have been disposed of in the bay. It is possible that this disposal event involved a single barge-load of munitions; however, it may have involved considerably more. In 1933, the WPUMBA was reportedly uncovered by a strong hurricane, which led to a large waterfowl kill, where ducks supposedly "turned pink and died."

It is known that white phosphorus is a powerful systemic poison. It is absorbed through the skin, by ingestion, and through the respiratory tract. The lethal dose (oral ingestion) in adult humans is about 1 mg/kg body weight, but as little as 0.2 mg/kg body weight may produce toxic symptoms. Skin contact produces severe and painful burns, with destruction of the underlying tissue. Inhalation of vapors has produced tracheobronchitis and liver enlargement.

However, because most sediments are anaerobic and are short distances below the water-sediment boundary surface, phosphorus degradation/oxidation may be extremely lengthy at such depths. Experiments determined that surface deposits of only a few ppm of phosphorus oxidize quickly, whereas deeper deposits of higher concentration could remain for years. Anaerobic sediments can, therefore, serve as sinks for white phosphorus that can, in turn, serve as long-term sources for mobilization of white phosphorus into the environment if disturbed [4].

Low concentrations of elemental phosphorus in the water column have been documented as causing acute effects on aquatic organisms. Fish appear more sensitive to the effects of white phosphorus than invertebrates. Another concern is the impacts of contamination through the food chain. Rapid bioaccumulation of white phosphorus has been documented and is related to the lipid content of the organism. Bioconcentration factors of between 20 and 100 have been reported for aquatic organism tissue.

White phosphorus contamination in various fish tissues has been shown to be toxic or lethal if ingested [5].

9.2   Pooles Island

Located onshore near Aberdeen, Maryland, at Pooles Island is a conical, 40-foot brick tower on a stone foundation; originally white with a black lantern. Originally the sound-signal building housed a fog bell. It was automated in 1917 and deactivated in 1939. Pooles Island Light now is located on the Aberdeen Proving Grounds and is closed to the public. The property was acquired by U.S. Army Garrison in 1917 and was used as an artillery range.

9.3   Berlin, MD

Berlin, Maryland, was a toxic smoke testing site. Most of the toxic smoke candles contained arsenic. Large quantities of arsenicals were tested and/or buried at the site, from which arsenic can easily enter the groundwater. A smoke candle consisted of a five-pound tin cylinder looking very much like a kitchen canister for flour or sugar. It had an igniting mechanism under the lid which was struck much like a highway flare.

Although this site drains into the Atlantic Ocean, not into the Bay, its contaminants may nevertheless find their way into Bay fish and waterfowl. There is also the question of where the leftover smoke candles were dumped.

Several comprehensive works on WWI ordnance and chemical warfare indicate that between 3,000,000 and 4,000,000 toxic smoke candles were produced for a spring offensive slated to begin April 1, 1919. The purpose of these candles was to send clouds of poisonous smoke toward the German trenches. Due to Brownian motion, smoke could penetrate the best of gas masks in WWI. However, we discovered that if the mask canister was placed in a half inch felt bag, it would filter out the arsenic if the wind shifted.

Some of these smoke candles were likely stored at Edgewood Arsenal and the chemical weapon vaults at Norfolk. What became of them is somewhat of a mystery, but dumping in the Bay and offshore in the Atlantic Ocean is likely.

TOXIC SMOKE CLOUD FROM 300 D.M. CANDLES

The candles were placed in three parallel rows
each containing 100 candles on a 100 yard front
and were ignited one row at a time at intervals of
3 or 4 minutes. Although wind conditions were un-
favorable, the Standard Box Respirator and German
Canister were penetrated at distances of at least
a mile. Unprotected observers on the edge of cloud
2800 yards from origin coughed severely.

Test near Berlin, Md., Nov.2, 1918.

PLATE XXII

Figure 9.7 The D.M. abbreviation in the photo stands for Adamsite or
Diphenylaminechlorarsine. These are very toxic smokes which would leave
arsenic on the ground. The author's discovery of the Berlin, MD smoke candle
test photos led to the site being added to the Formerly Used Defense Site (FUDS)
inventory for future environmental work. Credit also goes to John Fairbank.

9.4   American University Experiment Station

The American University Experiment Station, is about one mile
from the Potomac River in Northwest Washington, DC. It is
included here because the site was the world's second largest
chemical weapons manufacturing, testing and experiment facility
in WWI. As the photograph indicates, there were over 150 buildings (see nos. 1–3, 5, 8). A companion facility named Camp Leach
(no. 9) trained thousands of soldiers in gas and flame warfare and
other WWI arts.

Over 1,000 shells and 500 bottles, many containing chemical warfare agent, have been excavated already. A large plume of

Figure 9.8 One of the 140 laboratories at the American University Experiment Station making poison gas (1917–1918).

Figure 9.9 Haber nitrogen fixation furnaces (one under construction) in rear (1917-1918). These ran twenty-four seven making large quantities of nitrogen used for explosives.

perchlorate exists in the groundwater left over from the American University Experiment Station. This perchlorate contaminated groundwater reaches the Potomac and also the C&O Canal. Four-thousand shells in 14 burial pits have still not been found according to historic information.

Figure 9.10 This Lewisite still blew up, gassing U.S. Senator Scott. Later a fraternity house was located on the site. A child conceived there had double-club feet and a fraternity brother developed scrotal cancer at age 26. Next a Child Development Center was built on the site for the children of the American University staff and professors. This site was first questioned by reporter Harry Jaffe and investigated by the author. The arsenic on the surface where the children had their garden and played with their Tonka Toys had over 400 parts per million (ppm) arsenic. At five feet it was 2500 ppm.

Figure 9.11 Small-scale poison gas manufacturing stills.

"Today, [there are] more than 100 million metric tons of nitrogen fertilizer produced through the Haber-Bosch process....In his 2001 book *Enriching the Earth*, Vaclav Smil, a distinguished professor of geography at the University of Manitoba, Canada, calls it 'the single most important change affecting the world's population–its expansion from 1.6 billion people in 1900 to today's 6 billion–would not have been possible without the ability to synthesize ammonia'....

"Smil estimated that about 40 percent of the global population owed their very existence to the Haber-Bosch process, without which they would starve.

"But the process has been a mixed blessing for humanity, Smil noted....The ready availability of fertilizer also caused a huge amount of nitrogen to be released into the environment, leading to eutrophication in coastal waters such as the Chesapeake Bay...The Haber-Bosch process also has a dark side. Various forms of nitrogen are also critical to manufacture munitions [6]."

Circular trenches were used to test different gases on dogs. The trenches were circular so that it didn't matter what direction the wind was blowing on the day of a particular test. Dogs would be staked out and shells would be detonated in the middle of the circle. An empty jug would be placed in front of each dog and the concentration of gas, which would displace the lighter air in the jug, could be determined. Thus if a dog died at a given concentration and seven shells were detonated, it could be assumed that a similar volley of shells in Europe would kill men in the trench within x feet of the shells. The wires were used to statically fire the shells using a dynamite cap to set off the explosive. Most shells were detonated this way, as the mortars were too inaccurate to reliably hit the center of the trenches.

Figure 9.12 Circular trenches used to test different gases on dogs. Here a soldier is preparing a chemical shell for a static test. Extremely rare illnesses have been noted in seven homes that abut this trench.

Figure 9.13 Shell being detonated in a circular trench.

Figure 9.14 Mortars were used to fire large quantities of shells into the woods and fields near the Potomac River to test the shell fuzes and the spread of the gas. The cement angular Livens mortar platform on the left side of the photo found by Terry Slonecker, Greg Neilson, and the author, allowed the mortar range fan to be accurately determined. Several live shells were recovered from the mortar fan.

Figure 9.15 Toxic smoke or gas from mortar shells fired into an open field. Many of the gases contained arsenic and finding the areas still contaminated with arsenic nearly a hundred years later required testing the soil in 1400 front and back yards.

9.5   Patuxent River Chemical Incineration

Some chemical agents were incinerated at the Naval Air Station on the Patuxent River at the entrance to Chesapeake Bay. The nerve agents and lewisite were chemically neutralized [7].

9.6   Langley

Langley was first used to test chemical bombs during WWI as an adjunct site for the American University Experiment Station, the world's second largest chemical weapons manufacturing, development, and test facility at the time.

9.7   Naval Research Laboratory – Chesapeake Bay Detachment

The Chesapeake Bay Detachment of the Naval Research Laboratory (NRL) occupies a 168-acre site near Chesapeake Beach, Maryland, and provides facilities and support services for research in radar, electronic warfare, optical devices, materials, communications, and fire research.

Figure 9.16 This photo of Dr. Herbert Friedman with an Aerobee rocket illustrates that the Chesapeake Bay detachment experimented with rockets. As such, pollutants from rockets, such as perchlorate, may exist on site.

However, in the past it has served as an artillery range, bombing range, and chemical weapon burn site. During wartime expansion, NRL carried on the most extensive activities in its history.

In 1946, NRL directed the development of a new sounding rocket called Viking, and a total of 12 Viking rockets were launched from 1949 to 1954.

NRL worked with the Applied Physics Laboratory to develop a scientific rocket called Aerobee, as a replacement for the German V-2s that were being used for research following World War II.

"The NRL is a great research laboratory with the mission to develop guns [and] new explosives [8]."

9.7.1   Dumpsite Containing 150 Tons of Lewisite Near NRL [9]

In this event, 150 tons of lewisite were dumped in Chesapeake Bay. Lewisite was the deadliest gas invented, but never used, in World War I. Lewisite was extremely feared. Many rumors surrounded it. It was called the "Dew of Death" as a single drop on a man's skin was said to be fatal. The joke of the day was that if you put three drops on the tongue of a dog, it would kill the owner. It could penetrate rubber boots. The Japanese reportedly used Lewisite and mustard to kill a quarter million Chinese in the Iching Peninsula just before WWII.

The lewisite saga began with a top-secret program to manufacture it during World War I. The gas was invented by Captain W. Lee Lewis at Catholic University, in 1918. A secret plant was established to manufacture it at Willoughby, Ohio. The first batch of 150 tons was in route to Edgewood Arsenal when the war ended (November 11, 1918). It traveled on a train like no other. Only the engineer aboard the train was from the railroad, the rest of the crew where soldiers. The train went no faster than ten miles per hour. It took four days for it to get to Edgewood Arsenal, and by then the war was over.

In his book, *Gas Warfare*, Brigadier General Alden H. Waitt states, "A plant for its manufacture was constructed at Willoughby, Ohio, and a quantity was manufactured. This plant was called The Mousetrap because the product was so secret that the men who were engaged in making the first lots could not leave the premises….The Armistice took place before shipment of the first supply could leave port, and it was sunk at sea soon after the Armistice in order to destroy the gas [10]."

In their book, *A Higher Form of Killing*, Robert Harris and Jeremy Paxman state, "The first batch of 150 tons of Lewisite was at sea, on its way to Europe when the Armistice was signed [11]."

Edward M. Spiers in the book, *Chemical Warfare*, states, "The first 150 tons of Lewisite was at sea, en route to Europe, when the armistice was signed [12]."

However, this does not end the problem. "Sea" is a little word that covers a big area. The *San Francisco Journal*, February 19, 1923 stated, "At last the makers decided to sink the cylinder containing it in the waters of Chesapeake Bay, on the theory that it would disintegrate so gradually that no harm would be done." Lewisite was still cloaked in secrecy when this paper was published and the quantity produced (150 tons) was not known. In a speech by Captain Lewis on November 21, 1921, he states that after the explosion of the Lewisite Plant at American University, the War Department used the explosion as an excuse to say that lewisite would not be produced. He could not even tell his team, who were depressed by the false story, that a large plant was built to produce lewisite in Willoughby, Ohio. That plant had at least 40 tons of lewisite on hand when the armistice was signed, and that may have been dumped into Lake Erie.

In a translation of an editorial in a French publication, *ARBETAREN,* dated January 12, 1926, the following is stated, "As early as the next year [1918] the United States had such a large supply of Lewisite that the united armies of Europe might have been annihilated with it....After the war, the greater portion of the poisonous gas was destroyed (this is believed to be in Chesapeake Bay)...." The editorial continues, "In trying to bore a hole in a safe in a bank in Chicago, three burglars were killed by a gas streaming out of a metal bottle in the safe. This gas was Lewisite and two milligrams, that is only two thousandths of a gram, were sufficient to kill three men." This paper also refers to a later dump in 1926 of six chests in the Atlantic Ocean. This material was believed to have been the production run after the train left Willoughby and before the War ended.

Time magazine, February 1, 1943, honored Captain Lewis when he died. It stated, "Because no one knew what to do with it, the U.S. supply of lewisite was dumped in the sea off Baltimore after the Armistice."

Other sources suggest that the lewisite was dumped 50 miles from Baltimore [13] [14] [15]. Since the Chesapeake and Delaware Canal was too shallow at the time to take 150 tons of anything through it, the shipment had to go south. One internet site, no longer available, stated that it was in 516 steel drums.

Fifty miles ends right in the middle of the largest "dead zone" in the Bay. Not so strangely, charter boat captains do not take their clientele there to catch rockfish. The 50-mile line also ends at one of the deepest portions of the Bay channel, about 95 feet. That line also coincides with a military warning zone for the Naval Research Laboratory.

The Chesapeake has other contamination and dangers from past military dumping. A one-ton cylinder of mustard gas was dumped in the northern part of the bay and radioactive pellets were strewn on the bottom of the Bush River. Shells from the ranges at Aberdeen Proving Ground (Edgewood Arsenal) were buried near the shore and are now eroding out of the little cliffs, or dumped in a nearby creek. Also, bottles of mercury recently eroded out of the little cliffs along Aberdeen. Lewisite was dumped near Kings Creek.

It is believed that the mustard cylinder was dumped in the upper Bay during the trip to dump three barges because it started leaking. Being dumped in he 1960s in the upper Bay indicates that the barge went through the Chesapeake and Delaware canal.

Oysters in the Chesapeake Bay have been found to contain arsenic [16].The authors concluded that the source was environmental but left open the primary source. (Note: they did not sample oysters in the vicinity of 50 miles from Baltimore.) Naturally occurring arsenic is very low on the east coast, usually 1–3 ppm in the soil. Since Lewisite was also dumped off the coast of South Carolina, 1507 tons in March 1958, this could be one source. Lewisite is one-third arsenic by weight, thus even if it has broken down by now, that would still amount to 50 tons of arsenic in Chesapeake Bay.

Lewisite remains in our chemical weapons arsenal today, even after the discovery of the nerve agents such as sarin and VX.It causes severe damage at 1 part per million in the air over time. It is instantly lethal at 250 parts per million. There is evidence that it has similar lethality for fish since their gill structure is similar to our lungs [17].In fact, blue gills are used to test for trace amounts of chemical warfare agent in water because they are so sensitive, much like the canary in the mine. None live in Aberdeen's ground water.

No one can estimate how many fish, crabs, oysters and clams have succumbed to the poisons dumped in the bay. As these containers breech, sea life in the vicinity will certainly be killed. Efforts should be made to locate these munitions and remove them or encapsulate them in concrete.

It has been determined that lewisite in its L-1 form (2-Chlorovinyl arsonous dichloride) readily hydrolyzes to 2-chlorovinylarsonous acid (and hydrochloric acid), and then to lewisite oxide, a particularly toxic degradation product [18].

When examining the environmental fate of numerous chemical weapons agents, including lewisite, sulfur mustard, VX, GB, GA, GD and cyanogen chloride, it was shown that lewisite oxide was among the most persistent and maintained the characteristic of higher mammalian toxicity [19].

In portions of the Chesapeake Bay watershed elevated arsenic concentrations were observed in ground water with low dissolved oxygen content. Under these reducing conditions, arsenic could be mobilized from the reduction of metal oxides [20].

Though previous opinions focused on inorganic arsenic species as toxic, and the consequent methylation pathways as essentially detoxifying steps, evidence now points to the contrary, i.e., both inorganic and organic forms are toxic, though the mechanism for toxicity in each is different [21].

Marine algae are capable of transforming arsenate into non-volatile methylated compounds MMA and DMA, in seawater, and though arsenate is known to disrupt protein phosphorylation and the protective methyl groups of DNA, methylated arsenicals also induce DNA hypomethylation affecting numerous gene expression changes and consequent carcinogenesis [22] [23].

Factors confounding the study of arsenic toxicity stem from an indication that DNA methyltransferase activity, which is attenuated with chronic arsenic exposure, may not be the only factor in arsenic-induced DNA hypomethylation [24].

Lastly, it is also well-established that arsine gas is a potent hemolytic agent, though its lifetime is comparitvely short, and it is readily converted back to a water-soluble species [25].

Though arsenic bioaccumulation in the food chain and concentration in drinking water have been the primary focus of study, the variety of toxic mechanisms in almost any arsenic species suggests that the presence of a long-term arsenic sink in a natural system is potentially disastrous. The wide range of seasonally-driven pH, oxygenation, microbial activities and reduction-oxidation conditions that exist in the Chesapeake Bay may make it difficult to assess the fate and mobility of anthropogenic sources of arsenic. However, reducing and eliminating exposure to arsenic hotspots should be prioritized.

In addition to the use of methods to test for inorganic and organic arsenic in biota of marine and terrestrial origin, site-characterization and remediation technologies for unexploded ordnance-contaminated underwater sites should be continued using the advancing technologies available with autonomous underwater vehicles and equivalent emerging technologies [26].

9.8   Washington Navy Yard

Documents in the National Archives indicate that chemical warfare material was also sent to the Washington Navy Yard, including gas grenades and smoke mixtures, and may be present in disposal/fill areas. Smoke mixtures for navy smoke funnels at that time probably were either a bromine compound or titanium tetrachloride, since either has toxic properties. Gas grenades at the time of the shipments were most likely stannic chloride.

9.9   Tidewater Community College – Suffolk

A 1993 Army report details unexploded munitions found at Tidewater Community College, Suffolk, and reveals the discovery of what may have been chemical warfare agents. Signs on the campus warn of unexploded ordnance.

9.10   Other Hampton Rhodes, Norfolk, Virginia Beach Sites

There was a former Navy dive-bombing range in Virginia Beach, known as Naval Air Station Creeds. A sign still reads, "Warning. Bio chemicals. Keep out. Gas mask eye protection required [27]."

During WWI enormous quantities of chemical munitions and bulk agent were shipped overseas from Edgewood Arsenal. Some, no doubt, were simply loaded on barges and sent to the Norfolk area depots, since supply ships were in short supply. Thus a convoy could save time by not navigating up the Chesapeake, but could load in Norfolk and set sail for France immediately. This could save a week of time as the Bush River depot was too small to accommodate six or eight ships at a time.

The author advised on the cleanup of one such chemical weapons storage site in Norfolk that had brick-lined bunkers with drain lines to help remove any leaking agent.

A federal document on sea-dumped munitions includes the following references:

> **V1** Seven shiploads of chemical munitions were thrown into the sea near the Virginia-Maryland border off the Eastern Shore during one week in September 1945. Dumped were 75,852 mortar shells filled with mustard gas and 924 white phosphorous cluster bombs, which could contain as many as 60 smaller munitions each. More than 1,000 55-gallon steel drums of arsenic trichloride—which in small doses damages the nervous system and can cause genetic mutations—were also dumped, as were an estimated 23,000 chemical smoke projectiles. The Coast Guard cutter Gentian and several amphibious landing ships did the dumping.

V2 On Nov. 13 and 14, 1957, the USS Calhoun County loaded 48 tons of lewisite at Colts Neck Naval Pier in Earle, N.J., and dumped it off the continental shelf in 12,600 feet of water off Virginia Beach.

V3 In 1960, the Army dumped 317 tons of unidentified radioactive waste and two 1-ton containers of lewisite in deep water off Chincoteague.

V4 In 1964, the Army used the same location to dump 800 55-gallon drums of some kind of radioactive waste, along with 74 1-ton containers of mustard agent and 1,700 mustard-filled artillery shells.

V5 In 1962, more than 200 tons of radioactive waste in steel barrels was dumped within a few miles of the 1960 dump zone, along with 700 mustard-filled artillery shells and 5,252 white phosphorous munitions.

X An unspecified type and quantity of chemical munitions might have been dumped somewhere off Norfolk or Virginia Beach during World War II. The only known surviving record of the sea-dumped chemical weapons says they came from "Nanseman" depot, which likely was the Nansemond Ordnance Depot in Suffolk. The unconfirmed dumpsite was somewhere in "the Atlantic Ocean" near the mouth of the Chesapeake Bay [28].

While some of the dumps (i.e. **V2**) are deemed well offshore by the depth of the water, others are more questionable. For example, **X** is near the mouth of the Chesapeake, and some of the agent in **V1** was dumped using amphibious landing ships, which would seem to be dangerous to take a hundred miles offshore fully loaded. As noted in the Elinor logbook, drums (and presumably one-ton cylinders of agent) can float because air space is left in them for expansion protection.

Finally, clamming operations are clearly going far offshore now and are finding chemical shells from some dumps. Also, shells are being pumped in during beach replenishment operations.

References

1. Downloaded 02-04-2013 from: www.themilitarystandard.com/army_base/md/apg.php - Cached
2. Center for Land Use Interpretation Archive ID#: MD3136

3. Ted Wheeler & Mark Rindler, www.dtic.mil/ndia/2002training/rindler.pdf
4. Downloaded 08-22-2012 from: www.techbastard.com/army_base/md/apg.php - EPA/ROD/R03-91/126 1991.
5. Ibid.
6. bay journal may 2012. karl blankenship. downloaded 11/16/12 from: www.bayjournal.com/article/converting_nitrogen_in_air_to_usable...
7. www.stormingmedia.us/keywords/LANDFILLS-4.html -
8. star.nesdis.noaa.gov/star/.../Day1/Paul_Stewart_NRL_day1.pdf
9. Robert Johnson, MD, researched and wrote much of this subchapter.
10. Brigadier General Alden H. Waitt, *Gas Warfare, Chemical Warfare Service*, New York: Duell, Sloan and Pearce, 1944, pg. 55.
11. Harris, R., and Paxman, J., *A Higher Form of Killing*, Hill and Wang, New York, pg.32.
12. Spiers, E.M., *Chemical Warfare*, University of Illinois Press, Urbana and Chicago, pg. 36.
13. Evans, R., *Gassed!*, House of Stratus, London, 2000.
14. Stockbridge, F.P., *Yankee Ingenuity in the War*, Harper Brothers, New York, 1920.
15. Vilensky, J.A., and Sinish, P.R., Lewisite: Production, use, dumping and destruction, Indiana University School of Medicine, 2004.
16. Riedel, G.F., and Valette-Silver, N., Differences in the bioaccumulation of arsenic by oysters from Southeast coastal US and Chesapeake Bay, *Chemosphere* 49(1):27–37 Oct. 2002.
17. Opresko, D.M., et al., Chemical warfare agents: Estimating oral reference dose, *Environ. Contam. Toxicol.* 156: 1–183 1998.
18. Waters, W.A., Williams, J.H., Hyrdolyses and derivatives of some vesicant arsenicals, *J. Chem. Soc.* 1950, 18–22.
19. Munro, N.B., Talmage, S.S., Griffin, G.D., Waters, L.C., Watson, A.P., King, J.F., and Hauschild, V. The sources, fate, and toxicity of chemical warfare agent degradation products. *Environ. Health Perspect.* 1999 Dec;107(12):933–74.
20. Hancock, T.C., Denver, J.M., Riedel, G.F., and Miller, C.V., Reconnaissance for arsenic in a poultry dominated Chesapeake Bay Watershed–Examination of source, transport, and fate, U.S. Geological Survey.
21. *Toxicol. Appl. Pharamcol.* 2004 Dec 1;201(2):156–65.
22. *Rev. Environ. Contam. Toxicol.* 1992;124:79–110.
23. *Environ. Health Perspect.* 2004 Aug;112(12):1253–63.
24. *Toxicol. Appl. Pharmacol.* 2005 Aug 15;206(3):288–298.
25. *Toxicol. Appl. Pharmacol.* 1989 Jan;97(1):173–82.
26. Department of Defense, Strategic Environmental Research and Development Program (SERDP), *Anal. Bioanal. Chem.* (2003) 377:6–13.
27. Downloaded 11/16/12 from: www.treasurenet.com/forums/treasure-news/48349-unexploded-bombs..., 2007, *Daily Press*.
28. Downloaded 11-29-12 from: www.dailypress.com/media/acrobat/2005-10/20226301.pdf

10

Military Facilities Grouped by Specific Areas or on Specific Rivers

10.1 Potomac River

In *Poisoned Waters*, Hedrick Smith, one of America's most distinguished journalists, speaks with researchers from the U.S. Geological Survey (USGS), who report finding genetically mutated marine life in the Potomac River. In addition to finding frogs with six legs and other mutations, the researchers have found male amphibians with ovaries and female frogs with male genitalia. Scientists told *FRONTLINE* that the mutations are likely caused by exposure to "endocrine disruptors," chemical compounds that mimic the body's natural hormones [1].

10.1.1 Various Military Facilities

Various military facilities drain into the Potomac River drainage basin including Fort Detrick. Because of the research into biological agents at this site, various agents and decontamination chemicals probably contaminated the groundwater. For example, "5,000 bombs containing anthrax spores were produced at the base during World War II [2]." In addition, Fort Detrick's water and waste water treatment plants comprise about 16 acres on the banks of the Monocacy River which drains into the Potomac River.

Fort Belvoir, Virginia, has had a mixed use for many years. SM-1 was a 2-megawatt nuclear reactor developed by the United States Atomic Energy Commission for the U.S. Army Nuclear Power Program (ANPP) in the mid-1950s. In WWI, an Army gas school was established at Fort Belvior, then called Camp Humphreys. Photos in the National Archives show soldiers firing gas mortars there. Its close proximity to the American University Experiment Station and the adjacent Camp Leach made this an ideal location.

10.1.2   Old Navy Radio Station

The old Navy Radio Station in Arlington, Virginia, was the site of early radio experimentation around 1918. It was next to Fort Myer. Large antenna towers were the predominate structures. The site had two large septic tanks. When they hooked up to a new sewer system for the city, the abandoned septic tanks were filled with refuse around 1935 according to a historical report from the Navy archives. These septic tanks drained into a little creek that runs into the Potomac, instead of into a septic field. It is likely that lead, mercury, and other contaminants from early electrical equipment were dumped into these tanks. A drawing exists precisely locating these septic tanks, now on the grounds of the Defense Logistics Agency.

In 1918, Fort Myer had a portion of the 75 mm gun battery that was stationed across the river from Camp Leach in the District of Columbia. After the war, this battery remained there for ceremonial purposes. It was adjacent to the Navy Station property.

In 1993, a Civilian Conservation Corps worker reported that these two pits were filled in with 75 mm shells. Whether these contained mustard or other chemical weapons material or were simply high explosive shells is unknown. This same worker had also reported burying 14 pits of shells at the American University Experiment Station (AUES) in Spring Valley, Washington, DC. His report is deemed credible by the District of Columbia Government in part because he identified some of these shells as French 75s with mustard. Very few people knew that our WWI 75 mm chemical shells were developed from the French 75; and that a lot of experimentation work on the French 75 shells was conducted at the AUES and that 1200 mustard-filled 75 shells were on hand when the war ended.

Figure 10.1 Explosive cannonballs stacked up at the Washington Arsenal.

10.1.3 Washington Arsenal

The Washington Arsenal also sat on the banks of the Potomac River. It is believed that many of these cannon balls shown in Figure 10.1 were later dumped into the river when they became obsolete. Sampling in an old adjacent canal, now filled in, has found high levels of lead probably from Civil War era mini-balls dumped in the canal.

10.1.4 Naval Air Station

The site of the Naval Air Station located on the Potomac River shows an extensive history dating back to WWI. In addition, the army had Bolling Field, now Bolling Air Force Base. There was also the Naval Belvue Annex which produced munitions. There were three large earthen-bermed magazines that stored shells and bombs.

Finally, the leftover munitions were removed in 1964, as the memo from the Naval Station commander shown in Figure 10.2 indicates. (The memo is included as a photograph because it shows the casual nature of munitions disposal.) Nothing in the memo indicates where the munitions were disposed. (See Section 2.3, James Dolph, *2010 Navy Responses to DDOE Comments on Potential Historical Munitions Issues at the Washington Navy Yard.*)

NS/216:1e
5750

d. Rear Admiral A. J. HILL, Commandant of the former Potomac River
Naval Command, has his headquarters at the Washington Navy Yard of the
Naval Station. His command became Naval District Washington, Washington,
D. C., on 1 January 1965.

e. Some unusual events or accomplishments by the Naval Station in 1964
are listed below.

(1) In January, cataloging of surplus optical blanks was completed
and reported to the Defense Logistics Service Center for sale. This
material, valued at $1,250,000, was the largest declaration of excess
material submitted to the Center by this station.

(2) In August, at the request of the Chief of Industrial Relations,
the Consolidated Industrial Relations Office, U. S. Naval Station, sponsored the First Washington, D. C. International Relations Field Institute,
subsequently categorized as outstanding.

(3) Disposal of 3,975 items of heavy ordnance, valued at
$30,839,639, was accomplished under the Bureau of Weapons disposal program
during 1964. At the close of the year, the inventory of heavy ordnance
had been reduced to $556,529 in value.

(4) As of 1 December 1964, most of the functions of the Household
Goods Division were transferred to the Consolidated Household Goods Shipping Office, Cameron Station, Alexandria, Virginia.

(5) The Navy Exchange Department opened a Retail Store and a Cafe-
teria at the Washington Navy Yard Annex in 1964.

(6) The Presidential yachts HONEY FITZ and PATRICK J were deactivated in September 1964.

(7) In November, Mr. Paul B. Fay, Under Secretary of the Navy, made
a surprise inspection of the enlisted barracks at the Arlington Annex of
the Naval Station. The result was a letter of commendation to the Comman-
ding Officer for excellence of barracks maintenance.

2. The Naval Station maintains a detailed history of events of note con-
cerning the present station and the former Receiving Station dating back to
1952 in book form under the title "Station Journal".

H. F. ROMMEL

Figure 10.2 Naval Station commander memo that illustrates the casual nature of munitions disposal.

10.1.5   Naval Surface Warfare Center, Indian Head

"At the time of our visit, officials at the Naval Surface Warfare Center, Indian Head, in Maryland, reported they detected perchlorate contamination at five sites on the installation, of which three were landfills, one was a metal parts disposal site, and one was a metal parts degreasing tank site. Indian Head detected maximum perchlorate concentrations between 88 and 450,000 parts per billion in the soil at two of the three landfills. At the third landfill, a perchlorate concentration of 2,000 parts per billion was detected in the groundwater [3]."

Founded more than 100 years ago in 1890, the facility at Indian Head was the Navy's first established presence in Southern Maryland. What began many years ago as a gun test facility on the Potomac River has since evolved and expanded to include numerous scientific and response-force missions serving the Navy, Air Force, Army, and Marines. From its 3,400-acre peninsula, Naval District Washington, Indian Head, is home to several large tenant commands including the Indian Head Division, Naval Surface Warfare Center, the Naval Explosive Ordnance Disposal Technology Division, the Naval Ordnance Safety and Security Office, the Naval Sea Logistics Center, the Marine Corps Chemical Biological Incident Response Force, and the Joint Interoperability Test Command.

Naval Powder Factory, Indian Head, developed and successfully tested a 4.5-inch AA rocket in 1941. This type of rocket would have had perchlorate as a fuel.

10.1.5.1   Stump Neck Annex

The Stump Neck Annex is on a peninsula south of Indian Head. The mission of the Naval Explosive Ordnance Disposal Technology Division is to develop procedures for rendering safe weapons, missiles, and munitions. The Naval Explosive Ordnance Disposal (EOD) School provides training in methods and procedures for recovery, evaluation, rendering safe, and disposal, of explosive ordnance (surface, underwater, conventional, and nuclear types). The Stump Neck Annex is bordered on the north and east by Mattawoman Creek and Chicamuxen Creek [4]. The problem is that explosive contaminants (munitions constituents or MCs) can enter the creeks, then the Potomac River and then the Bay.

10.1.6   Dahlgren

"In 1844 the U.S. Navy decided to show off their newest acquisition, a steam-powered, propeller-driven war ship with a 12-inch experimental gun. On February 28, President John Tyler, members of Congress, newspaper reporters and other guests boarded the USS Princeton at the Washington Navy Yard. The group enjoyed a leisure cruise down the Potomac while the Princeton demonstrated her maneuvering ability and armament. On the return trip the ship passed Fort Washington as Captain Robert F. Stockton prepared to fire one last round from the 12-inch, 225-pounder gun called 'Peacemaker.' When fired, the gun burst wounding many guests and killing five observers including Navy Secretary Gilmer, Secretary of State Upshur and a Congressman.

"A Board of Inquiry found that no person could be held responsible for the mishap but they did find fault with the gun. They also concluded that the [then-current] technology could not produce a safe large gun. Large gun manufacturing ceased and for a while it seemed that ship builders had won the war against the gun [5]."

Admiral John A. Dahlgren of the U.S. Navy believed that manufacturing guns with thicker metal at the breach would solve the problem. His scientific approach to gun design necessitated a testing range originally called the Pentcote Battery after the name of the little stream where it was located. Later, his work was moved to the current site on the Potomac River.

In designing his big guns it was necessary to test fire them, hence a river range was created. Dahlgren's outdoor mission activities take place on the Potomac River Test Range and Explosives Experimental Area. "Dahlgren's first mission at the end of World War I—*testing ordnance*—continues today, although it is only part of what they do now. Because our sailors live, work, and sleep next to explosives, they need to know that ammunition won't explode by accident. And we need to know that the guns our people handle will work as designed, not backfire or misfire. To be certain about the guns and ammunition we send out with our troops, the Navy tests everything at Dahlgren before it reaches our ships. We use the Potomac River Test Range to develop and test guns, ammunition, and weapon systems components and to evaluate new weapons and sensors [6]."

Dahlgren's mission has changed and/or increased over the years. From the highlights below, several missions creating an environmental concern are evident. For example, proofing of guns by firing shells and development of bombs left thousands of tons of unexploded ordnance in the river and Bay. Work on rockets left perchlorates and other fuels in the surface and groundwater.

> **1921–30** Work mainly concerns proofing of large caliber naval rifles, but also in areas of exterior ballistics, aerology, velocity, range table production and calculations.
>
> **1930** Special ballistics investigations through experimental department leads to creation of Armor and Projectile Laboratory to explore ballistics, heat treating, metallographics, chemistry and spectochemistry of projectiles and armor.

1943 AA Fuse and Machine Gun Ranges established.

1944 Pumpkin Neck Test Area acquired giving Dahlgren a total acreage of 5,422.847. Dahlgren ordnance expertise tapped for ultra-secret Manhattan Project then ongoing at Los Alamos, NM. Dahlgren learns its role in triggering device.

1950 Korean War; work on new guns and rockets begins at Dahlgren. Work begun on Elsie (MARK 8 and 91 bombs) projects.

1959 Naval Proving Ground, Dahlgren, renamed Naval Weapons Laboratory.

1960 NWL begins work on guided projectiles and rockets; Dahlgren experiences rapid development [7].

NSWC-Dahlgren is approximately 4,300 acres and located 40 miles south of Washington, DC, along the Potomac River. This naval facility, established in 1918, conducts research, development, testing, and evaluation of surface ship weaponry. Activities at Main Side, a 2,678-acre area include air operations, ordnance testing, laboratory testing, computer facilities, administrative offices, and residences. The Explosive Experimental Area (EEA), is an isolated testing range located on 1,614 acres. Both areas are separated by the Upper Machodoc Creek.

The Navy has identified several sources of contamination at NSWC-Dahlgren. The Fenced Ordnance Burial Area (Site 2) was used for burial of excess munitions, in addition to several nearby trenches filled with wastes, and has metals detected in the surface soils. The Terminal Range Airplane Park (Site 6) was an area used to store target materials, and is contaminated with heavy metals and polyaromatic hydrocarbons (PAHs). The Disposal/Burn Area (Site 9), a two to three acre landfill, is contaminated with PAHs, and the soils and sediment contain phenols, metals, and pesticides waste. Site 9 is a threat to the groundwater as well as to the wetlands that surround the landfill. Hideaway Pond (Site 10) contains sediment and fish contaminated with mercury. The Chemical Burn Area (Site 12) was used for decontamination of testing materials and has 1,1,1 trichloroethane (TCA) in the alluvial aquifer below the site. The Chemical Waste Evaporation Pond (Site 14) was used for the disposal of decontaminated chemicals from 1967 until the late 1970s. The 1400 Area Landfill (Site 17), five to ten acres in size, received municipal waste for three years in the

1970s, and canisters of mercury may have been disposed of in this area. Low levels of mercury were detected in groundwater underlying Site 17 and in stream sediments nearby. The Transformer Draining Area (Site 19), where electrical transformer oil containing polychlorinated biphenyls (PCBs) was drained, has PCB contamination to a depth of four feet. The Former Electroplating Waste Underground Storage Tank (Site 20) has minor solvent contamination in the groundwater. The Pesticide Rinse Area (Site 25), where pesticide containers were rinsed, is contaminated with pesticides. The Lead Contamination Area (Site 37) contains used sand from firing ranges with residual heavy metals as contaminants. Landfill A: Stump Dump Road (Site 46), used in the 1940s and 1950s for general disposal, has PAH, PCB, and heavy metal contamination. The Fill Areas Northeast EEA (Site 50) is a small burial dump that has PAH and heavy metal contamination. The Gambo Creek Ash Dump (Site 61), where residual ash was deposited, may contain heavy metals, especially mercury, and is in contact with sediments in Gambo Creek. There are also six sites that are related to the former use of munitions, including depleted uranium and explosives.

Figure 10.3 Firing 14-inch gun at Dahlgren Proving Ground.

Figure 10.4 Transportation personnel at Naval Support Facility Dahlgren prepare to off-load a World War I-era tractor-mounted artillery piece, the first gun originally test-fired to mark the establishment of Dahlgren as a naval proving ground on October 16, 1918.

Figure 10.5 Made around 1899 at Watervliet Arsenal in New York, this big 12-inch gun is still capable of firing. After arriving at the Naval Proving Ground in Dahlgren, it was used for the ballistic testing of bombs.

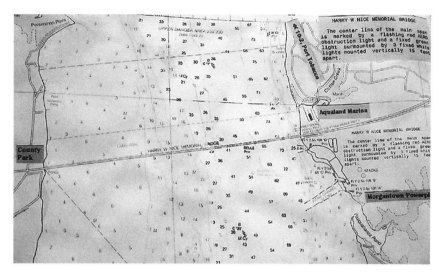

Figure 10.6 Dahlgren chart listing Upper Danger Area.

Figure 10.7 The Dahlgren bone yard has an impressive array of discarded armament including this 24-inch smooth bore gun.

Figure 10.8 During World War II women served in gun crews at Dahlgren to ensure the Navy could sustain intense range tests in support of the war effort in spite of labor shortages.

Figure 10.9 A 16-inch battleship gun is fired during proof tests on Dahlgren's main range. The base's large-caliber range is used to proof *every* naval gun before it is installed on a ship. "The 16-inch (406 mm) is the biggest and required this Potomac River location to have a 20 mile test range for the gun. Its range is 27 miles. Fishermen are ordered off the river for testing. The 16-inch was last tested for projectiles used on the Iowa in Desert Storm [8]."

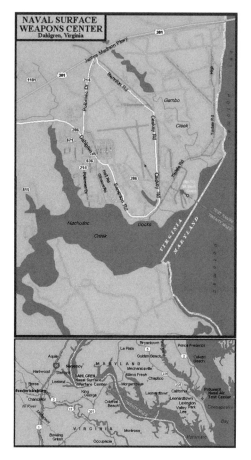

Figure 10.10 Dahlgren has a 20 mile range for projectile testing. Shells are piled four feet deep undoubtedly contributing to the Potomac River's high nitrogen content [9].

10.1.7   Newtowne Neck State Park

"Growing up, George E. Raley Jr. heard stories that the military had conducted some sort of testing during World War II on the quiet Southern Maryland peninsula known as Newtowne Neck. As an adult, he would learn that his father had assisted in experiments performed by the Johns Hopkins University Applied Physics Laboratory to develop a weapon credited with helping the Allies win the war in Europe. So he was not particularly surprised... when the sands of the peninsula where he once camped, swam and

Figure 10.11A 57 mm shell found on the beach at Newtowne Neck [11]. This shell has a proximity fuze which makes it extremely dangerous. Most metal detectors cannot be used to find such ordnance for fear of setting it off.

picked blackberries shifted to reveal a small but substantial stock-pile of World War II-era munitions….

"Authorities, alerted by a local woman who came across a 57 mm ammunition round while strolling on the beach…have found 27 pieces of suspected military ordnance along the shoreline of what is now Newtowne Neck State Park [10]."

The point of the above anecdotes is that the military has used land for munitions training and testing that it never owned or even leased. Thus munitions can be found anywhere. Note that the live shell shown in Figure 10.11 is fuzed. It is likely that this is a proximity fuze, since Johns Hopkins had some role in the development of this fuze. If so, it is a very dangerous fuze and could be detonated by using a two-way radio or a metal detector.

10.2   Anacostia River

10.2.1   The Washington Navy Yard on the Anacostia River

The Washington Navy Yard is the oldest Naval facility in the country. It sits on one of the ten most polluted rivers in the nation (by some accounts it is the worst polluted river). Indeed, the Navy Yard has caused much of that pollution.

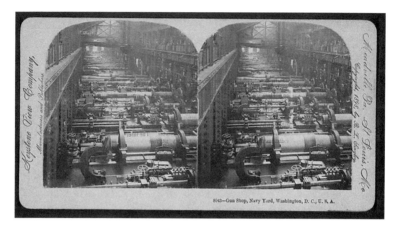

Figure 10.12 Navy Yard Gun Shop, Washington DC (1898).

Figure 10.13 Navy Yard Breech Mechanism Department, Washington DC (1898).

Since the District of Columbia is not a heavy manufacturing city, the Navy Yard serves as one of its few heavy industrial sites. For over two centuries, it has been a shipyard, foundry and naval gun factory. Some of the contaminants found at the Navy Yard and in the river adjacent to it are as follows:

Chemicals and Metals Found in Fish Tissue Studies

Also Found in Navy Yard Groundwater/ Sediments
(WP Tables B-3, B-6, B-9, B-12, B-17, B-19, B-20,B-22)

Metals 1992 Fish Study	Metals Found at Navy Yard
As	arsenic
Hg	mercury
Be	beryllium
Cd	cadmium
Cr	chromium
Pb	lead
Ni	nickel
Ag	silver
Tl	thallium

Fish not Tested for	barium
"	cobalt
"	manganese
"	potassium

Volatiles 1992 Fish Study	Volatiles Found at Navy Yard
methylene chloride	methylene chloride
1,1,1-trichloroethene	1,1,1-trichloroethene
1,2-dichloroethane	1,2-dichloroethane

Semi-volatiles 1991 Fish Study	Semi-volatiles Found at Navy Yard
anthracene	anthracene
fluoranthene	fluoranthene
naphthalene	naphthalene
phenanthrene	phenanthrene
pyrene	pyrene
bis(2-Ethylhexyl)phthalate	bis(2-Ethylhexyl)phthalate

	Not Yet Found in Navy Yard GW/Sed
phenol	"
acenaphthylene	"
aceanaphthene	"
diethylphthalate	"
fluorene	"
di-n-butylphthalate	"

Pesticides 1991 Fish Study	Not Yet Tested for in Navy Yard GW/Sed
Heptachlor	"
Heptachlor epoxide	"
a-Endosulphan	"
Dieldrin	"
pp'-DDE	"
Endrin	"
b-Endosulphan	"
pp'-DDD	"
Endrin Aldehyde	"
Endosulfan Sulfate	"
pp'-DDT	"
y-chlordane	"
a-chlordane	

Polycyclic Aromatic Hydrocarbons 1993, 1994, 1995 Fish Study	Found in some Navy Yard Samples
benzo[a]anthracene	benzo[a]anthracene
chrysene	chrysene
benzo[b]fluoranthene	benzo[b]fluoranthene
benzo[k]fluoranthene	benzo[k]fluoranthene
benzo[a]pyrene	benzo[a]pyrene
indeno[1,2,3-cd]pyrene	indeno[1,2,3-cd]pyrene
dibenzo[a,h]anthracene	dibenzo[a,h]anthracene
benzo[g,h,i]perylene	benzo[g,h,i]perylene
Not Tested for in Fish	**Found in some Navy Yard Samples**
"	fluorine
"	acetone
"	carbon disulfide
"	benzene
"	chloromethane
"	bromomethane/ chlorethane
"	fluorotrichloromethane
"	1,1-dichloroethane
"	t-1,2-dichloroethene
"	1,1-dichloroethane
"	carbon tetrachloride

"	trichloroethene
"	1,2-dichloropropane
"	bromodichloromethane
"	2-chloroethyl vinyl ether
"	c-1,3-dichloropropene
"	t-1,3-dichloropropene
"	1,1,2-trichloroethane
"	chlorodibromomethane
"	chlorobenzene
"	bromoform
"	1,1,2,2-tetrachloroethane
"	3-dichlorobenzene
"	1,2-dichlorobenzene
"	1,4-dichlorobenzene
"	ethyl benzene
"	toluene
"	xylene

Many fish in the Anacostia River have lesions. As many as 70 percent of the brown bullheads may have lesions. This fish is particularly telling since it does not travel more than a half mile from where it is hatched. Thus any contamination or environmentally-related disease that it has is acquired locally, probably from one or more of the contaminants listed for the Navy Yard. Similar contaminants from other military facilities likely explain the growing number of Rock Fish with lesions in the Bay.

Figure 10.14 Photo showing a lesion (cancerous growth) on a fish.

10.2.1.1   Ordnance

Experimental work on ordnance became a major mission of the Navy Yard. Its name was changed to the U.S. Naval Gun Factory at one point. The gun factory was actually established in 1799 as a small portion of the activity. Samuel Colt who developed the revolver, also experimented with electrically fired mines. Robert Fulton was one of the first to develop underwater mines. In the Civil War a large percentage of 50 Union ships were damaged or sunk by mines. The Washington Navy Yard was active in this development and manufactured large quantities of ordnance [12].

Prior to the invention of the radio, one primary method of signaling from ship to ship or even from unit to unit in the Army was the use of signal pistols and rockets. The Navy Yard pioneered these methods. The signaling chemicals used were often toxic.

Following the Civil War, the yard continued to be the scene of technological advances. In 1886, the yard was designated the manufacturing center for all ordnance in the Navy. Ordnance production continued as the yard manufactured armament for the Great White Fleet and the World War I Navy. The 14-inch naval railway guns used in France during World War I were manufactured at the yard.

During WWI, "…projectiles, mines, fuzes, pyrotechnics…were other projects of this period [13]."

Figure 10.15 The U.S. Navy Model 1861 and U.S. Army Model 1862 percussion signal pistols made at the Navy Yard.

By World War II, the yard was the largest naval ordnance plant in the world. The Navy Bureau of Ordnance established a facility for testing rocket motors at the Naval Gun Factory, Washington, DC, in 1943 [14].

The weapons designed and built at the Washington Navy Yard were used in every war in which the United States fought until the 1960s. At its peak, the yard consisted of 188 buildings on 126 acres of land and employed nearly 25,000 people. Small components for optical systems and enormous 16-inch battleship guns were all manufactured here. In December 1945, the Navy Yard was renamed the U.S. Naval Gun Factory. Ordnance work continued for some years after World War II until finally phased out in 1961. Three years later, on July 1, 1964, the activity was redesignated the Washington Navy Yard. The deserted factory buildings began to be converted for office use [15].

Early on, on September 7, 1841, an explosion during an ordnance experiment at the Washington Navy Yard killed two workers. For safety purposes, the laboratory and powder magazine were then moved to separate locations [16]. The widow of a worker killed in another explosion at the yard during WWI became the first female employee of the yard sewing powder bags. The gun powder may well have been produced at the adjoining Washington Gas Light Site, which still contains large areas with a high level of dinitrotoluene, an explosive in Navy bag powder.

Figure 10.16 View of the northwestern part of the Washington Navy Yard, looking eastward, 1866.

10.2.2   Experimental Battery

The Experimental Battery at the Washington Navy Yard test fired ordnance. Historical reports from the Battery indicated that they fired into the mudflats across the river and down river past Geisboro Point. The Battery mud flats impact area likely encompassed some of the current Naval Air Station property. Live ordnance (likely from this Battery) has recently been found on the Naval Air Station. About 15 years ago another live shell was found at Bolling AFB. Historical Still Photographs and paintings depict the Experimental Battery at the Navy Yard.

Fuzed shell were fired so that experimental shell could be recovered and examined for performance assessments if they failed to detonate. Note: A Civil War Shenkle round was found on *Bolling* property. It was deemed too dangerous to move, as this round contained an early impact fuze mechanism (musket cap) and was blown in place. It is unknown whether this was from the Experimental Battery or from Rebel fire across the river.

There were also three eprouvette mortars, still on the grounds of the Navy Yard, that were used to test the tremendous quantities of gunpowder supplied to the Navy. While the ordnance fired by these mortars was shot not shell, faulty powder was dumped, along with any leftover black powder, when the guns changed to breach loading using smokeless powder bag powder.

"The eprouvette was a variation of the mortar. As seen in Figure 10.17, construction was a simple 'cup' on a fixed bed. Elevation was exactly 45 degrees. Based on that fixed elevation, the strength of

Figure 10.17 An eprouvette mortar. Photo: Craig Swain (July 21, 2008).

the powder could be calculated based on the distance a 24 pound shot was propelled by a single ounce of powder. The range was expected to exceed 225 yards. Good powder propelled the shot to over 300 yards.

"The eprouvette fell into disfavor as it was discovered black powder strength increases exponentially as quantity is increased. Furthermore, the qualities of slow burning powder, which worked much better in long bore cannon, could not be tested in the small mortar [17]."

The site of the Experimental Battery was moved to the grounds of the U.S. Insane Asylum (now St. Elizabeth's Hospital) during the remainder of the war. It was renamed the Pencote Battery after the creek where it was located.

One final event bears noting. According to the *Washington Star*, January 24, 1954, 15 million pounds of 5-inch shell casings were smelted down at the Navy Yard. There is always residual unburned powder (likely a nitroglycerine and nitrocellulose mixture) in empty shell casings. In addition, the primer compounds could be fulminate of mercury or lead azide with antimony sulfide. These munitions constituents (MCs) are likely to remain as contaminants, given the large quantity of shell casings that were processed.

Figure 10.18 This is believed to be an 11-inch shell probably weighing 900 lbs. Solid non-explosive shot of this size are unusual since the shell is so heavy that it would penetrate most armor-plated ships, and thus if it exploded it would do much more damage.

Recently ordnance has been excavated from a former part of the Navy Yard now in private hands. Some have been three-inch shells that were live.

10.3   Severn River

Base regulations describe needing exclusive jurisdiction of an area in the River for experiments. This area consists of the waters of the Severn River shoreward of a line beginning at the southeastern-most corner of the U.S. Navy Marine Engineering Laboratory sea wall and running thence southwesterly perpendicular to the main Severn River channel, approximately 560 feet, thence northwest-erly parallel to and 50 feet shoreward of the edge of the channel, 1,035 feet, and thence northeasterly perpendicular to the channel, approximately 600 feet, to the shore. Spar buoys will mark the corners of the area adjacent to the channel.

(b) *The regulations.* (1) No vessel or person other than specifi-cally authorized military and naval vessels and persons shall enter or remain in the area during its use for experimental purposes (see Appendix I). It is unknown what types of experiments were done or what contaminants may have been left.

Further government documents describe rocket testing. The Navy Engineering Experiment Station in Annapolis, MD, was directed to undertake the development of liquid-fuel rocket JATO for large flying boats. A PBY Catalina, fitted with two liquid-pro-pellant JATO rockets developed at Annapolis, took off with 20 per-cent reduction in run [18].

10.4   Norfolk (Hampton Rhodes Area)

See Appendix IV for a listing of 174 military facilities in the Norfolk-Hampton Rhodes Area compiled by John Bull and associates.

In the past, every section of Virginia has been a battleground of some sort or another. The modern military bases in the state are located along the Fall Line or in Tidewater. If Congress authorized one more military base in the Norfolk area, it might cause Virginia to tilt up on its side and sink into the Atlantic Ocean [19], [20], [21].

Norfolk was a naval shipyard in WWI, but was in decline after the war to end all wars. That is, until WWII, when Norfolk expanded to become our biggest naval base. Together with Portsmouth and Newport News, the Hampton Roads area converted into a giant war machine. The population of Norfolk swelled from 119,000 to 222,000 people.

As one can easily imagine, shipyards are notorious polluters. Heavy metals, asbestos, oil, slag, coal, PCBs and other substances find their way into the water. Navy yards also have munitions, chemical warfare material, and explosives.

Hampton Rhodes also was a staging area for shipments of ordnance and chemical warfare material overseas. During recent environmental restoration efforts, a brick-lined subterranean warehouse was found complete with floor drains. It did not take much ingenuity to realize that this was a holding area for drums of chemical warfare material and chemical ordnance coming from the WWI Edgewood Arsenal. For example, in 1946, the Naval Mine Depot at Norfolk dispatched a shipload of mustard projectiles to be dumped in the ocean.

One of the problems at the Hampton Rhodes area is the standard operating procedure of dumping unusable munitions in the water. Training Manual TM 9-1904 *Ammunition Inspection Guide* states, "The safest and easiest way to destroy unusable ammunition is to dump at sea."

According to John M.R. Bull and Stephanie Heinatz, "What once was isolated land is now prime – and potentially lethal – real estate [22]."

Figure 10.19 Nimitz-class aircraft carriers Dwight D Eisenhower (CVN 71) and Theodore Roosevelt (CVN 71) [23].

Figure 10.20 Guided-missile destroyer USS Donald Cook [24].

Recent photographs (Figures 10.19 and 10.20) bear witness to the active military use of the Chesapeake Bay. Even modern Naval vessels still leave pollution. Bottom paint, for example, often contains very toxic heavy metals. These toxins prevent the growth of barnacles and other marine life on the ship. While these have been removed from commercial products, this does not apply to the Navy.

10.4.1   Fort Wool

The range of land-based cannon (shore batteries) was inadequate to block the entrance to the mouth of the James River until Fort Calhoun (renamed Fort Wool in 1861) was constructed on the Rip-Raps shoal between Hampton and Norfolk in the 1840–50s. Starting in 1819, the Americans sought to fortify the natural reef about halfway between Hampton and Norfolk. Mounds of granite from quarries near Baltimore were piled onto the Rip-Raps, but the heavy stones sank into the soft sediments.

"Rip-Raps got its name from the rippling of the water, as the Chesapeake Bay encountered a shallow shoal off the Peninsula. After seven years of reinforcing the shoal with heavy stone, the army began construction of Fort Calhoun on the new man-made island. Robert E. Lee's first assignment after graduating from West Point in 1829 was to serve as an engineer on that project [25]."

A mock fire control station was established in the mine command station on top of the old fort, with two M1910A1 azimuth instruments, the TI bell, and two EE-91 telephones connected through the switchboard to several other phones located in the magazine (Figure 10.21). The visitors were able to use the instruments to track ships and observe tourists visiting the 3-inch guns of Battery Erwin at Fort Monroe, and speak to other visitors in the magazine using the EE-91 telephones. Of course, the fire control towers were used to practice the shelling of targets in the Bay and off the coast. This triangulation apparatus was placed in the large concrete towers like the one shown in Figure 10.22.

Figure 10.21 Mock fire control station in the mine command station.

Figure 10.22 Fire control tower from Cape Delaware.

10.4.2   James River

The ghost fleet, a group of WWII destroyers, was moored in the James River. Navy ships have their electrical switches encased in oil to prevent them from corroding in salt air. This oil in WWII contained Polychlorinated Biphenyls (PCBs). These switches had gaskets which eventually leaked, allowing the oil to seep into the bilge. The ghost fleet was also outfitted with battery-operated automatic bilge pumps to evacuate rainwater and other water that leaked into the bilge. These pumps also discharged the PCBs into the river. The PCBs got into the menhaden, a silvery fish, which among other things, are exported to Scotland to feed farmraised salmon. Now these farmed salmon have high levels of PCBs.

PCBs tend to concentrate in the fatty part of the fish, and accumulate in the oil.

"What's the deal with fish oil?" Paul Greenberg asks in his op-ed piece, "A Fish Oil Story."

He goes on to say, "If you are someone who catches and eats a lot of fish, as I am, you get adept at answering questions about which fish are safe, which are sustainable, and which should be avoided altogether. But when this fish oil question arrived in my inbox recently, I was stumped. I knew that concerns about overfishing had prompted many consumers to choose supplements as a guilt-free way of getting their omega-3 fatty acids, which studies show lower triglycerides and the risk of heart attack. But I had never looked into the fish behind the oil and whether it was fit, morally or environmentally speaking, to be consumed.

"The deal with fish oil, I found out, is that a considerable portion of it comes from a creature upon which the entire Atlantic coastal ecosystem relies, a big-headed, smelly, foot-long member of the herring family called menhaden, which a recent book identifies in its title as *The Most Important Fish in the Sea* [26], [27] ."

10.4.2.1   Nansemond Ordnance Depot

Nansemond Ordnance Depot, 975 acres of land formerly used as an Army ammunition depot located in Suffolk, Virginia, is located along the James River by the Monitor-Merrimac Memorial

Bridge-Tunnel. Ordnance and raw explosive were dumped into the river and Bay. Nansamond Ordnance Depot ultimately became the site of Tidewater Community College.

A 1993 Army report details unexploded munitions found at Tidewater Community College in Suffolk and reveals the discovery of what may have been chemical warfare agents [28].

Figure 10.23 Aerial view of the former Nansemond Ordnance Depot. *The Virginia Engineer* © IIr Associates 2005.

Figure 10.24 Bulk TNT at Nansemond Ordnance Depot. John Bull notes that over 2,000 pounds of TNT have been found in the area, brown and crystallized.

Figure 10.25 A 16-inch gun at Fort Story [29].

10.4.2.2   Fort Story

Joint Expeditionary Base East (formerly known as Fort Story as a sub-installation of Fort Eustis), is a sub-installation of the United States Navy and Little Creek Amphibious Base. It is located in the independent city of Virginia Beach, Virginia, at Cape Henry at the entrance of the Chesapeake Bay. It had two 16-inch guns.

References

1. Adam Shake, Poisoned Waters – Frontline Examines the Chesapeake Bay and Puget Sound, on *Frontline*, PBS, Hedrick Smith.
2. GAO report number GAO-04-601, supra.
3. Retrieved September 8, 2010 from www.globalsecurity.org/military/facility/nrl.htm
4. *www.globalsecurity.org/military/systems/ship/steam6.htm*
5. http://www.navsea.navy.mil/nswc/dahlgren/EIS/EIS-to-Date/Mission_Focus.aspx
6. www.dcmilitary.com/special_sections/sw/081206z.shtml
7. Downloaded 12-18-12 from: ships.bouwman.com/Navy/Dahlgren/index.html
8. Ibid.
9. Downloaded 08-20-2012 from: articles.baltimoresun.com/keyword/fort-belvoir by Matthew Hay Brown, January 21, 2012.

10. Downloaded 09-05-2012 from: www.dnr.state.md.us/publiclands/southern/newtowne.asp - Cached

11. Downloaded 02-04-2013 from: www.nps.gov/fowa/historyculture/torpedo.htm - Cached

12. Newsletter, *U.S. Naval Gun Factory*, September 1949, pg. 8.

13. Retrieved September 8, 2010, from history.nasa.gov/Timeline/1940–44.html

14. History of the Washington Navy Yard Department of the Navy -- Naval Historical Center, 805 Kidder Breese Se -- Washington Navy Yard Washington Dc 20374-5060.

15. www.ibiblio.org/hyperwar/NHC/accidents.htm - 182k - Cached

16. Submitted: August 6, 2008, by Craig Swain of Leesburg, Virginia

17. Retreived September 8, 2010 from: history.nasa.gov/Timeline/1940–44.html

18. The Military in Virginia, www.virginiaplaces.org/chesbay/chesat-tack.html -

19. General Accounting Office, DOD Lacks a Comprehensive Plan to Manage Encroachment on Training Ranges

20. (GAO-02-614), June 2002, p. 12 Downloaded 11/16/12 from: www.treasurenet.com/forums/treasure-news/48349-unexploded-bombs...

21. articles.dailypress.com/.../news/...roads-bombing-ranges - Cached, The Daily Press June 03, 2007, Bombs Left Behind

22. Photo from the sailing catamaran Minnow, August 2006 xpda.com/chesapeake -

23. Ibid.

24. Downloaded 09-05-2012 from: virginiaplaces.org/chesbay/chesat-tack.html - Cached

25. Franklin, H.B., *The Most Important Fish in the Sea: Menhaden and America*, Island Press, 2006.

26. Greenberg, P., A fish oil story, *The New York Times*, published: December 15, 2009

27. Bull, J.M.R., and Heinatz, S., Bombs left behind, *Daily Press*.

28. Downloaded 08-27-12 from: en.wikipedia.org/wiki/Fort_Story - Cached

11

Radioactive Contamination

Strontium 90 has been found in the drinking water for the District of Columbia (see *Setting an Environmental Agenda,* U.S. EPA Region 3 May 9, 1996). The District of Columbia gets its drinking water from the Potomac River, thus anything from the river, including in its sediments, is also likely to enter the Bay.

Strontium 90 is not a naturally-occurring radioactive isotope, as is, for example, radon. Strontium 90 is a fission product. Most likely, its source is a nuclear facility far upstream on the Potomac River.

In the 1950s, drums of "atomic waste" were dumped off the Atlantic Coast.

In 1960, 317 tons of unidentified radioactive waste was dumped off Chincoteague. In 1962, 200 tons of radioactive waste in steel barrels was dumped off Chincoteague. In 1964, (800) 55-gallon drums of unspecified radioactive waste was dumped. All originated from the Aberdeen Proving Ground (see *Cleanup of Chemical and Explosive Munitions,* 2012 Elsevier UK). More recently, pellets of radioactive thorium nitrate were dumped in the Bush River.

Dumping of radioactive material off the coast would not seem to affect the Bay. However, this material constitutes heavy metals and as such is easily taken up by filter feeders such as clams. When

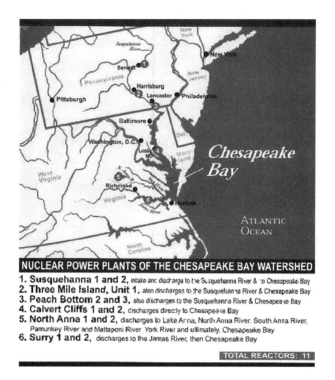

NUCLEAR POWER PLANTS OF THE CHESAPEAKE BAY WATERSHED

1. **Susquehanna 1 and 2,** intake and discharge to the Susquehanna River & to Chesapeake Bay
2. **Three Mile Island, Unit 1,** also discharges to the Susquehanna River & Chesapeake Bay
3. **Peach Bottom 2 and 3,** also discharges to the Susquehanna River & Chesapeake Bay
4. **Calvert Cliffs 1 and 2,** discharges directly to Chesapeake Bay
5. **North Anna 1 and 2,** discharges to Lake Anna, North Anna River, South Anna River, Pamunkey River and Mattaponi River York River and ultimately, Chesapeake Bay
6. **Surry 1 and 2,** discharges to the James River, then Chesapeake Bay

TOTAL REACTORS: 11

Figure 11.1 Chesapeake Bay Watershed nuclear power plants.

a clam dies, it is most likely eaten by a fish that could migrate into the Bay. Worse, the clam may be caught and processed for seafood, with wastewater (and probably sludge) a necessary byproduct, likely finding its way into the Bay. And, the now radioactive clamshell could be dumped in a driveway anywhere in the Bay drainage area. Of course the author still loves New England clam chowder.

It is unknown how much radioactive waste has been buried or leached out within Aberdeen itself, but large quantities have been transported there as shown by the tonnage sent from Aberdeen for ocean dumping.

While the nuclear waste is not specified, it is believed to be spent reactor fuel. Most spent fuel rods still have an extensive half-life, 12,000 years not being uncommon.

"Government regulations allow radioactive water to be released to the environment containing permissible levels of contamination. *Permissible does not mean safe.* A typical 1000-megawatt pressurized-water reactor (with a cooling tower) takes in 20,000 gallons of river, lake or ocean water per minute for cooling, circulates it through a 50-mile maze of pipes, returns 5,000 gallons per minute to the same body of water, and releases the remainder to the atmosphere as vapor. A 1000-megawatt reactor without a cooling tower takes in even more water—as much as one-half million gallons per minute. The discharge water is contaminated with radioactive elements in amounts that are not precisely tracked, but are potentially biologically damaging [1]."

Other reactors included one at Fort Belvoir and one at Walter Reed Medical Center, either of which could have emitted radioactive waste into the Potomac River.

References

1. Map and quote downloaded 11/23/12 from: www.nirs.org/factsheets/chesapeakepam.pdf

12

PCB and Other Ship Contamination

12.1   Navy Use of Polychlorinated Biphenyls

Polychlorinated biphenyls (PCBs) comprise a type of oil used for decades to cool and insulate electrical transformers, capacitors, and electrical switching components. PCBs are a class of organic compounds with 1 to 10 chlorine atoms attached to a biphenyl, which is a molecule composed of two benzene ring structures. These dielectric fluid compounds are highly toxic to humans. These compounds have been illegal since 1979. They do not break down readily, and are persistent contaminants in the environment.

The Navy used PCBs in tremendous quantities because many switches on ships were encased in PCB oil to keep them from corroding in the salt air. Eventually the neoprene seals around the switches began to leak and the oil ran down into the bilge of the ship only to be pumped out.

The lower James River is contaminated from PCBs from the ghost fleet, comprised of Navy ships mothballed at anchorage in the event of future need. The ships were installed with automatic bilge pumps to remove rainwater that accumulated in their bilges. Unfortunately the PCBs contained in the electrical equipment on

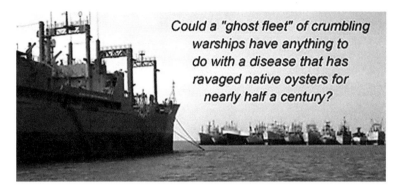

Could a "ghost fleet" of crumbling warships have anything to do with a disease that has ravaged native oysters for nearly half a century?

Figure 12.1 The James River Fleet. Photograph: Michael W. Fincham.

board also dripped into the bilge water and were discharged overboard when the pumps kicked in.

"The James River Reserve Fleet, often called the Ghost Fleet, dates back to 1925. By 1950, it held 800 ships, many of them reactivated for the Korean, Vietnam, and first Gulf wars. Like the oyster, the fleet has dwindled—only 57 now remain [1]."

Unlike other oil, PCBs sink in water and accumulate in sediment. Here they can be ingested by various insects and taken up by aquatic plants, and absorbed by bottom-dwelling fish such as eels, catfish, and bullheads.

Most contaminants escalate up the food chain. Thus a top predatory fish like rockfish, generally contain larger amounts of contamination than smaller fish. Mercury contamination in tuna for example, is well known.

In the case of PCBs, bottom-dwelling fish and fatty fish contain more PCBs. In samples of fish caught in the Anacostia River, near the Washington Navy Yard, and Potomac River, near the Naval Research Laboratory, The maximum concentration of PCBs in a fish sample was 2.60 parts per million (ppm), which was detected in a composite of fillets from three eels. In channel catfish composites, the highest PCB concentration was 2.00 ppm, and in largemouth bass, 0.062 ppm. Fish consumption advisories exist for fish caught in DC waters and for those caught in Maryland and Virginia waters below DC. See Appendix X for tables indicating species and advisories.

A few years ago, the amount of PCBs in farm-raised salmon from Scotland came to the attention of the US Food and Drug Administration (FDA). Since these fish were raised in relatively pristine waters, the source of the PCBs puzzled some. It turned out that the salmon were fed menhaden caught on the lower Chesapeake Bay, near the James River. These menhaden were full of PCBs from the ghost fleet and presumably other sources. These small fatty fish are also pressed for oil contained in some vitamin and fish oil caplets.

Babies born to women who ate PCB-contaminated fish also showed abnormal responses in tests of infant behavior. Some of these behaviors, such as problems with motor skills and a decrease in short-term memory, last for years. The immune system is also affected in children born to and nursed by mothers exposed to increased levels of PCBs. PCBs alter estrogen levels in the body and contribute to reproduction problems in women. PCBs are also classified as probable human carcinogens by the National Cancer Institute, World Health Organization, and the Agency for Toxic Substances and Disease Registry as they are associated with liver and breast cancer.

The extensive use of PCBs aboard Navy ships also caused another problem not normally associated with electric power company use of PCBs. When working on shipboard switches, any leaked PCB fluid had to be wiped up with rags, as it was an oil and made decks slippery. The oily rags would typically be burned at incinerators located on Navy shipyards where the repairs were made. Typically these incinerators did not supply oxygen to the combustion chamber and the PCBs were transformed into dioxins, and even more toxic substance. A wind plume of dioxins from the site of the incinerator at the Washington Navy Yard has been found to spread even to Capitol Hill.

Figure 12.2 Abandoned Navy ship showing PCB-containing electrical fixtures.

Figure 12.3 Navy ship PCB-stained electrical panel.

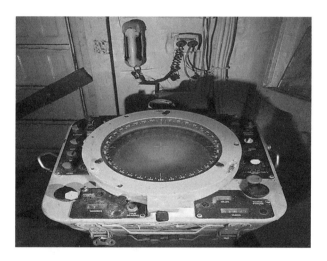

Figure 12.4 Oil-immersed phone jack on an abandoned Navy ship.

Environmental distribution of dioxins is global. Dioxins are found throughout the world in practically all media. The highest levels of these compounds are found in some soils, sediments and food, especially dairy products, meat, fish, and shellfish. Thus there is a body burden of dioxins in people. When localized contamination from a Naval facility is added to the the already existing dioxin body burden, the effect is worsened.

The Naval Research Laboratory on the Potomac River had a storage capacity of 148,800 gallons of PCB oil (dielectric fluid). While some of this could be used to refill leaking transformers or fill new transformers, much of it went to repair battle-damaged ships at the Washington Navy Yard. Indeed, the high level of PCBs in the sediments in front of the Washington Navy Yard attest to the discharge of PCBs from ship bilge water and other Navy sources, since PCBs do not migrate far from their deposition.

PCBs of course are used in electrical transformers owned by electric power companies. Under the pole transformers seen in suburban and rural areas, there is often a ring of oil-stained dirt around the pole. The pole transformers contain a drain plug with a neoprene seal. As the neoprene breaks down, the plug will leak. (Just like the oil drain plug on your older car will leave a drop on your driveway.) If the pole is old, that dirt is likely to contain PCBs. (Newer transformers also leak, but the oil does not contain PCBs.) Nevertheless, the PCBs in that oily ring are not likely to migrate into the water because PCBs are very sticky.

Of course, power company transformers in vaults in a city might well have drain lines into storm sewers. Here too a PCB leak will eventually get into the stream or river. At the Washington Navy Yard, the highest sediment level of PCB 12,000 μg/kg (aroclor 1260), was found at a storm sewer line that drained a large transformer vault in a Navy building. Three samples at the ends of the piers had 130, 130 and 120 mg/kg. A PCB sample upstream of the Washington Navy Yard had no exceedance. As high as these were, surface soil samples around Building 292 at the Navy Yard had PCB detections as high as 14,000 and 20,000 mg/kg.

A congener analysis was done on the PCBs in sediments at the Washington Navy Yard. This is an additional laboratory test designed to determine the exact molecular structure of the PCB molecule found. As noted above, there are many different chemical structures of the PCB molecule. In Washington, DC, the Navy used compounds that were different from the type used by the local power company. That way, it could be determined that the PCBs in the lower Anacostia River and the Potomac River by the Naval Research Laboratory were the Navy's, not the power company's.

For the Chesapeake Bay itself, PCBs are likely to be emanating from the Naval Research Laboratory, the Navy facilities at Norfolk,

Figure 12.5 Washington CVN-73 departing Chesapeake Bay for composite training.
Source: www.maritimequest.com

and any Navy piers at Baltimore. The Naval Research Laboratory had a burn pit located on site where they burned chemical agent and likely PCB-contaminated oil. Dioxins would also likely be present.

The Pentagon, although largely a huge office complex, has its own electrical supply and back-up systems. The electrical vaults are underground, but the floor drains are piped into a little bay off the Potomac River. When the transformer oil was primarily comprised of PCBs, they settled into this bay and severely polluted it. PCBs neither breakdown nor move, but they do find their way into aquatic organisms, particularly, fatty fish.

Navy ships have been so prevalent in the Chesapeake Bay that much of the PCB contamination found in the lower Bay can be attributed to those ships as a source.

"22 October 2003 (Geneva) – Four old US Navy ships being towed across the Atlantic to be scrapped in Britain are 'floating time bombs' carrying several hundred tonnes of hazardous waste, environmental groups warned on Wednesday.

"The rusting hulks contain about 350 tonnes of toxic chemicals (PCBs), 620 tonnes of asbestos and 470 tonnes of old fuel oil and represent a major pollution risk, the Basel Action Network (BAN), a network of groups including Greenpeace and Friends of the Earth, said.

"The first two ships left Chesapeake Bay on the US east coast two weeks ago and are being hauled in tandem by tugboats to northeastern Britain.... There are nine more ships ready to be sent to Britain and 150 old vessels from the US ghost fleet are slated for scrapping abroad... Some 450 ships have been sent for breaking in various countries in the world so far this year, Greenpeace said [2]."

References

1. *hesapeake Quarterly*, 2006, Volume 5, Number 2.
2. Downloaded 11/23/12 from: www.ban.org/ban_news/2003/031022_navy_bombs.html -

13

Environmental Justice

Any discussion insisting that the Federal Government clean up the federal pollution in the Chesapeake Bay would be incomplete without a discussion on environmental justice. Executive Order 12898 mandates an environmental justice assessment. Any strategy for cleaning the Bay developed by the Federal Government is void *ab initio* if it fails to account for the concept of environmental justice. Environmental justice is a concept that requires due consideration of impacts that both the problems and proposed solutions might have on minority and economically disadvantaged populations. Indeed, where any cleanup strategy addresses commercial harvesting of shellfish and fish, nearly all of these communities are environmental justice communities.

Environmental justice not only includes racial, religious, and ethnic minority populations but also economically disadvantaged populations. Small farmers and watermen generally fall into an environmental justice category. If, for example, governmental entities restrict the application of fertilizer to a farm field, mandate disposal of manure, or restrict the number of bushels of crabs or oysters that may be harvested daily, this has profound effects on the economically disadvantaged workers. Thus some means of amelio-rating the economic harm has to be part of the plan.

Even a federal committee organized under Executive Order ought to give credence to a congressionally authorized advi-sory panel, the National Environmental Justice Advisory Council (NEJAC). Indeed, the work of this committee was organized by the U.S. Environmental Protection Agency (EPA), which has adopted NEJAC's guidance. For another wing of EPA to vitiate NEJAC's findings is inexplicable, especially when recognizing some of the federal contribution to the Bay's decline.

Environmental justice issues regarding the Chesapeake Bay have been widely publicized for many years. Even the Chesapeake Bay Program features a section on its website regarding African American watermen. A popular book, *Exploring the Chesapeake Through Ebony Eyes,* by Vincent O. Leggett, has been around for sev-eral years. There even is an organization, Blacks of the Chesapeake Foundation, Inc., devoted to publicizing the minority history sur-rounding the Chesapeake.

Ironically, the very year that the Federal Leadership Committee drafted its plan for Chesapeake Bay, omitting mention of environ-mental justice, James McBride published his newest book, *Song Yet Sung.* This book memorialized the story of Harriet Tubman and her underground railroad, which relied heavily on the boats of black and white watermen to move escaped slaves around. Further, in December 2009, James McBride was interviewed for *Eastern Shore* magazine, and reminded us of a quote from Frederick Douglas. Mr. Douglas often said, "First of all, I am an Eastern Shore Waterman."

This same month, completion of the phenomenal quilt honoring black watermen was announced. It was unveiled December 9, 2009, at the Annapolis Maritime Museum and featured in the Capitol, December 17, 2009. It is difficult to understand why the Federal Leadership Committee missed so many contemporaneous clues about environmental justice.

And yet, when the Navy planned to resume use of the Bloodsworth Island Bombing Range, "Watermen [were] already saying they are concerned that if the Navy starts weapons practice on the islands, precious harvesting time [would] be lost and they [would] take another hit in an already ailing industry.

"'I'll have watermen who won't be able to feed their fami-lies,' said Ben Parks, president of the Dorchester County Seafood Harvesters Association and vice president of the Maryland

Watermen's Association. He said there are 100 families who he expects will be affected.

"Parks estimates that with the Navy proposing to use the islands for 1,200 hours a year, watermen will lose another 50 days of work on the water in that region of the bay."[1]

Indeed, it is a mystery why any federal agency would write *any* plan for the environment and not mention environmental justice. Failure to bring up the subject in a plan for the Chesapeake Bay, while blaming watermen for over harvesting of fish for part of the problem, suggests that the authors were not familiar with the Bay nor familiar with environmental restoration.

References

1. Downloaded 02-04-2013 from: www.newsline.umd.edu/.../bombing-balking030405.htm - Cached by Elizabeth A. Weiss and Sarah Lesher Capital News Service Friday, March 4, 2005.

14

Cleaning Up the Bay's Munitons

It is not an impossible task to clean up the bulk of the munitions in the Bay. The disposal sites are charted. The ranges are mapped. Several prominent target areas are also charted. These areas contain piles of bulk ordnance that could be easily removed. Hunting individual shells, bombs, and mines would be much more time consuming but these scattered ordnance items present much less of an overall threat to the Bay's ecosystem. The basic rule is, "Mine the High Grade Ore First."

Various detection devices can be used to find the large munitions piles:

- Sidescan sonar (See Figure 5.2)
- Underwater video cameras (towed from a boat)
- Ordinary sonar (fishfinders are now so good that shells are easily visualized)
- Underwater towed array metal detectors
- Underwater sniffers
- Underwater geiger counters

- Divers using scooters or being towed by boats on sleds
- In the past decade, two portable systems for the discrimination of unexploded ordnance (UXO) have been developed: the PINS system and the PELAN system. These might be useful on a range like Dahlgren where one could encounter solid shot or armor-piercing shot and high explosive (HE) or conventional rounds.

Once a large pile or target area is located, GPS can fix the position. Then robotic ordnance harvesters can be employed.

The option of exploding underwater ordnance where it is found presents other problems. "In addition to the toxicological threats, marine organisms, such as mammals or fish, can be hurt or even killed by the shock wave and the high sound pressure following an explosion. Harbor porpoises are killed within a distance of four kilometres from the explosion, their hearing can suffer permanent damage as far as 30 kilometers away."[1] While we don't have porpoises in the Bay, fish air bladders can also be damaged from explosive shock waves. Not to mention the toxic byproducts and sediment disturbances.

Other techniques can be employed but dangers also exist. "Gun cotton 39 bears a particularly dangerous potential when in contact with oxygen. Ammunition parts therefore need to be salvaged and removed when wet. It is, however, technically possible today to deactivate and cut ammunition using remotely controlled water abrasive suspension cutting (under water as well as above water), and it is technically feasible to burn the ammunition parts in water-filled containers in a mobile incinerator. The same applies to the removal of the explosives by flushing them out with warm water and treating them in an UV reactor. In such a reactor, explosive chemicals can be decomposed by much more than 99% under laboratory conditions, the rest being retained in activated-carbon filters."[2] Such reactors need more research.

Some of the Bay's WWI munitions likely contain gun cotton. "The earliest weapons (torpedoes) used wet gun-cotton."[3] Gun cotton HE artillery shells have also been found at the American University Experiment Station. Since WWI weapons were often discarded as being obsolete leading up to WWII, such gun cotton torpedoes could well be in the Potomac River or other disposal sites (see Figure 14.1).

Figure 14.1 Example of an obsolete 1,000-pound torpedo warhead discarded in Lake Michigan.

Figure 14.2 Army ROV clears underwater ordnance off Hawaii.[4]

For deeper water the harvester can be attached to a submerged robotically operated vehicle (SROV).

This harvester can be located on a platform for shallow areas like the 20 mile four-foot deep layer at the Dhalgren Range in the Potomac River, or it can be mounted on a tracked vehicle to move along the bottom in areas where the bottom is firm. The ordnance item can be lifted and deposited aboard a barge. The fuze can be cut off using a plasma cutter to make handling safer. The ordnance item can be burned right on the barge using small shaped cutting

Figure 14.3 Electromagnetic underwater ordnance harvester.[5]

Figure 14.4 A robotic ordnance harvester can be employed for safely removing munitions from the Bay's bottom. Several designs exist.

charges that burn a hole in the casing and which set the TNT or other filler on fire. A little air pollution is inordinately less problematic than the nitrogen entering the bay.

Since the methodology exists to clean up the Bay's ordnance hot spots, there is no good reason for delaying the effort.

Figure 14.5 An ordnance harvester (invented by Jim Barton) on an SROV lifts a 500-pound high-speed, low-drag bomb, like the two shown in Figure 5.2 that were found in the shipping channel by Jim Barton and Richard Albright II.

Conclusion

Efforts to clean up the Bay have failed for 20 years. The Bay is dying. Part of the failure is attributed to improperly designed cleanup plans that fail to sample the sediments in the Bay to help find the pollution sources that are in the Bay itself. These include munitions dumps, industrial waste dumps, and discharges from large ships, principally the Navy's mothballed fleet and major Navy shipyards. Even today, the Washington Navy Yard with the blessing of the EPA refuses to clean up the sediment contamination in the Anacostia River. Due to the narrow and shallow confines of the river, the amount of contaminated sediments would be very small.

Twenty million or so munitions have been fired or dropped into the Bay. Even assuming that only 10 percent still contain nitrogen or phosphorus compounds, it is still a tremendous continuing source of pollution. And this is a source that can largely be eliminated. Of course not every stray bomb or shell can be located, but the huge piles in disposal and target areas can be located and removed.

It is also worth mentioning that this mass of explosives and chemical weapons provides a handy source for terrorists.

Finally, the specific toxic substances in munitions are far more damaging to marine life and humans than are the phosphates in your dishwashing detergent or the fertilizer the farmer puts on the fields.

References

1. Downloaded 12-19-12 from: schleswig-holstein.nabu.de/naturvorort/meeressaeuger/...
2. Ibid.
3. Downloaded 12-19-12 from: www.navweaps.com/Weapons/WTUS_Notes.htm
4. Downloaded 12-19-12 from: ttmemedia.wordpress.com/category/green-tech/page/3
5. Downloaded 12-19-12 from: maic.jmu.edu/journal/7.1/focus/sprinkel/sprinkel.htm

Appendix I

Executive Order and Comments
Chesapeake Bay Protection and Restoration

By the authority vested in me as President by the Constitution and the laws of the United States of America and in furtherance of the purposes of the Clean Water Act of 1972, as amended (33 U.S.C. 1251 et seq.), and other laws, and to protect and restore the health, heritage, natural resources, and social and economic value of the Nation's largest estuarine ecosystem and the natural sustainability of its watershed, it is hereby ordered as follows:

Part 1 – Preamble

The Chesapeake Bay is a national treasure constituting the largest estuary in the United States and one of the largest and most biologically productive estuaries in the world. The Federal Government has nationally significant assets in the Chesapeake Bay and its watershed in the form of public lands, facilities, military installations, parks, forests, wildlife refuges, monuments, and museums.

Despite significant efforts by Federal, State, and local governments and other interested parties, water pollution in the Chesapeake Bay prevents the attainment of existing State water quality standards and the "fishable and swimmable" goals of the Clean Water Act. At the current level and scope of pollution control within the Chesapeake Bay's watershed, restoration of the Chesapeake Bay is not expected for many years. The pollutants that are largely responsible for pollution of the Chesapeake Bay are nutrients, in the form of nitrogen and phosphorus, and sediment. These pollutants come from many sources, including sewage treatment plants, city streets, development sites, agricultural operations, and deposition from the air onto the waters of the Chesapeake Bay and the lands of the watershed.

Restoration of the health of the Chesapeake Bay will require a renewed commitment to controlling pollution from all sources as well as protecting and restoring habitat and living resources, conserving lands, and improving management of natural resources, all of which contribute to improved water quality and ecosystem health. The Federal Government should lead this effort. Executive departments and agencies (agencies), working in collaboration, can use their expertise and resources to contribute significantly to improving the health of the Chesapeake Bay. Progress in restoring the Chesapeake Bay also will depend on the support of State and local governments, the enterprise of the private sector, and the stewardship provided to the Chesapeake Bay by all the people who make this region their home.

Part 2 – Shared Federal Leadership, Planning, and Accountability

Sec. 201. Federal Leadership Committee. In order to begin a new era of shared Federal leadership with respect to the protection and restoration of the Chesapeake Bay, a Federal Leadership Committee (Committee) for the Chesapeake Bay is established to oversee the development and coordination of programs and activities, including data management and reporting, of agencies participating in protection and restoration of the Chesapeake Bay. The Committee shall manage the development of strategies and program plans for the watershed and ecosystem of the Chesapeake Bay and oversee their implementation. The Committee shall be chaired by the Administrator of the Environmental Protection Agency (EPA), or the Administrator's designee, and include senior representatives of the Departments of Agriculture (USDA), Commerce (DOC), Defense (DOD), Homeland Security (DHS), the Interior (DOI), Transportation (DOT), and such other agencies as determined by the Committee. Representatives serving on the Committee shall be officers of the United States.

Sec. 202. Reports on Key Challenges to Protecting and Restoring the Chesapeake Bay. Within 120 days from the date of this order, the agencies identified in this section as the lead agencies shall prepare and submit draft reports to the Committee making recommendations for accomplishing the following steps to protect and restore the Chesapeake Bay:

a. define the next generation of tools and actions to restore water quality in the Chesapeake Bay and describe the changes to be made to regulations, programs, and policies to implement these actions;

b. target resources to better protect the Chesapeake Bay and its tributary waters, including resources under the Food Security Act of 1985 as amended, the Clean Water Act, and other laws;

c. strengthen storm water management practices at Federal facilities and on Federal lands within the Chesapeake Bay watershed and develop storm water best practices guidance;

d. assess the impacts of a changing climate on the Chesapeake Bay and develop a strategy for adapting natural resource programs and public infrastructure to the impacts of a changing climate on water quality and living resources of the Chesapeake Bay watershed;

e. expand public access to waters and open spaces of the Chesapeake Bay and its tributaries from Federal lands and conserve landscapes and ecosystems of the Chesapeake Bay watershed;

f. strengthen scientific support for decisionmaking to restore the Chesapeake Bay and its watershed, including expanded environmental research and monitoring and observing systems; and

g. develop focused and coordinated habitat and research activities that protect and restore living resources and water quality of the Chesapeake Bay and its watershed.

The EPA shall be the lead agency for subsection (a) of this section and the development of the storm water best practices guide under subsection (c). The USDA shall be the lead agency for subsection (b). The DOD shall lead on storm water management practices at Federal facilities and on Federal lands under subsection (c). The DOI and the DOC shall share the lead on subsections (d), (f), and (g), and the DOI shall be lead on subsection (e). The lead agencies shall provide final reports to the Committee within 180 days of the date of this order.

Sec. 203. Strategy for Protecting and Restoring the Chesapeake Bay. The Committee shall prepare and publish a strategy for coordinated implementation of existing programs and projects to guide efforts to protect and restore the Chesapeake Bay. The strategy shall, to the extent permitted by law:

a. define environmental goals for the Chesapeake Bay and describe milestones for making progress toward attainment of these goals;
b. identify key measureable indicators of environmental condition and changes that are critical to effective Federal leadership;
c. describe the specific programs and strategies to be implemented, including the programs and strategies described in draft reports developed under section 202 of this order;
d. identify the mechanisms that will assure that governmental and other activities, including data collection and distribution, are coordinated and effective, relying on existing mechanisms where appropriate; and
e. describe a process for the implementation of adaptive management principles, including a periodic evaluation of protection and restoration activities.

The Committee shall review the draft reports submitted by lead agencies under section 202 of this order and, in consultation with relevant State agencies, suggest appropriate revisions to the agency that provided the draft report. It shall then integrate these reports into a coordinated strategy for restoration and protection of the Chesapeake Bay consistent with the requirements of this order. Together with the final reports prepared by the lead agencies, the draft strategy shall be published for public review and comment within 180 days of the date of this order and a final strategy shall be published within 1 year. To the extent practicable and authorized under their existing authorities, agencies may begin implementing core elements of restoration and protection programs and strategies,

in consultation with the Committee, as soon as possible and prior to release of a final strategy.

Sec. 204. Collaboration with State Partners. In preparing the reports under section 202 and the strategy under section 203, the lead agencies and the Committee shall consult extensively with the States of Virginia, Maryland, Pennsylvania, West Virginia, New York, and Delaware and the District of Columbia. The goal of this consultation is to ensure that Federal actions to protect and restore the Chesapeake Bay are closely coordinated with actions by State and local agencies in the watershed and that the resources, authorities, and expertise of Federal, State, and local agencies are used as efficiently as possible for the benefit of the Chesapeake Bay's water quality and ecosystem and habitat health and viability.

Sec. 205. Annual Action Plan and Progress Report. Beginning in 2010, the Committee shall publish an annual Chesapeake Bay Action Plan (Action Plan) describing how Federal funding proposed in the President's Budget will be used to protect and restore the Chesapeake Bay during the upcoming fiscal year. This plan will be accompanied by an Annual Progress Report reviewing indicators of environmental conditions in the Chesapeake Bay, assessing implementation of the Action Plan during the preceding fiscal year, and recommending steps to improve progress in restoring and protecting the Chesapeake Bay. The Committee shall consult with stakeholders (including relevant State agencies) and members of the public in developing the Action Plan and Annual Progress Report.

Sec. 206. Strengthen Accountability. The Committee, in collaboration with State agencies, shall ensure that an independent evaluator periodically reports to the Committee on progress toward meeting the goals of this order. The Committee shall ensure that all program evaluation reports, including data on practice or system implementation and maintenance funded through agency programs, as appropriate, are made available to the public by posting on a website maintained by the Chair of the Committee.

Part 3 – Restore Chesapeake Bay Water Quality

Sec. 301. Water Pollution Control Strategies. In preparing the report required by subsection 202(a) of this order, the Administrator of the EPA (Administrator) shall, after consulting with appropriate State agencies, examine how to make full use of its authorities under the Clean Water Act to protect and restore the Chesapeake Bay and its tributary waters and, as appropriate, shall consider revising any guidance and regulations. The Administrator shall identify pollution control strategies and actions authorized by the EPA's existing authorities to restore the Chesapeake Bay that:

   a. establish a clear path to meeting, as expeditiously as practicable, water quality and environmental restoration goals for the Chesapeake Bay;
   b. are based on sound science and reflect adaptive management principles;
   c. are performance oriented and publicly accountable;
   d. apply innovative and cost-effective pollution control measures;
   e. can be replicated in efforts to protect other bodies of water, where appropriate; and
   f. build on the strengths and expertise of Federal, State, and local governments, the private sector, and citizen organizations.

Sec. 302. Elements of EPA Reports. The strategies and actions identified by the Administrator of the EPA in preparing the report under subsection 202(a) shall include, to the extent permitted by law:

a. using Clean Water Act tools, including strengthening existing permit programs and extending coverage where appropriate;
b. establishing new, minimum standards of performance where appropriate, including:
    i. establishing a schedule for the implementation of key actions in cooperation with States, local governments, and others;
    ii. constructing watershed-based frameworks that assign pollution reduction responsibilities to pollution sources and maximize the reliability and cost-effectiveness of pollution reduction programs; and
    iii. implementing a compliance and enforcement strategy.

Part 4 – Agricultural Practices to Protect the Chesapeake Bay

Sec. 401. In developing recommendations for focusing resources to protect the Chesapeake Bay in the report required by subsection 202(b) of this order, the Secretary of Agriculture shall, as appropriate, concentrate the USDA's working lands and land retirement programs within priority watersheds in counties in the Chesapeake Bay watershed. These programs should apply priority conservation practices that most efficiently reduce nutrient and sediment loads to the Chesapeake Bay, as identified by USDA and EPA data and scientific analysis. The Secretary of Agriculture shall work with State agriculture and conservation agencies in developing the report.

Part 5 – Reduce Water Pollution from Federal Lands and Facilities

Sec. 501. Agencies with land, facilities, or installation management responsibilities affecting ten or more acres within the watershed of the Chesapeake Bay shall, as expeditiously as practicable and to the extent permitted by law, implement land management practices to protect the Chesapeake Bay and its tributary waters consistent with the report required by section 202 of this order and as described in guidance published by the EPA under section 502.

Sec. 502. The Administrator of the EPA shall, within 1 year of the date of this order and after consulting with the Committee and providing for public review and comment, publish guidance for Federal land management in the Chesapeake Bay watershed describing proven, cost-effective tools and practices that reduce water pollution, including practices that are available for use by Federal agencies.

Part 6 – Protect Chesapeake Bay as the Climate Changes

Sec. 601. The Secretaries of Commerce and the Interior shall, to the extent permitted by law, organize and conduct research and scientific assessments to support development of the strategy to adapt to climate change impacts on the Chesapeake Bay watershed as required in section 202 of this order and to evaluate the impacts of climate change on the Chesapeake Bay in future years. Such research should include assessment of:

a. the impact of sea level rise on the aquatic ecosystem of the Chesapeake Bay, including nutrient and sediment load contributions from stream banks and shorelines;
b. the impacts of increasing temperature, acidity, and salinity levels of waters in the Chesapeake Bay;
c. the impacts of changing rainfall levels and changes in rainfall intensity on water quality and aquatic life;
d. potential impacts of climate change on fish, wildlife, and their habitats in the Chesapeake Bay and its watershed; and
e. potential impacts of more severe storms on Chesapeake Bay resources.

Part 7 – Expand Public Access to The Chesapeake Bay and Conserve Landscapes and Ecosystems

Sec. 701.(a) Agencies participating in the Committee shall assist the Secretary of the Interior in development of the report addressing expanded public access to the waters of the Chesapeake Bay and conservation of landscapes and ecosystems required in subsection 202(e) of this order by providing to the Secretary:

i. a list and description of existing sites on agency lands and facilities where public access to the Chesapeake Bay or its tributary waters is offered;
ii. a description of options for expanding public access at these agency sites;
iii. a description of agency sites where new opportunities for public access might be provided;
iv. a description of safety and national security issues related to expanded public access to Department of Defense installations;
v. a description of landscapes and ecosystems in the Chesapeake Bay watershed that merit recognition for their historical, cultural, ecological, or scientific values; and
vi. options for conserving these landscapes and ecosystems.

(b) In developing the report addressing expanded public access on agency lands to the waters of the Chesapeake Bay and options for conserving landscapes and ecosystems in the Chesapeake Bay, as required in subsection 202(e) of this order, the Secretary of the Interior shall coordinate any recommendations with State and local agencies in the watershed and programs such as the Captain John Smith Chesapeake National Historic Trail, the Chesapeake Bay Gateways and Watertrails Network, and the Star-Spangled Banner National Historic Trail.

Part 8 – Monitoring and Decision Support for Ecosystem Management

Sec. 801. The Secretaries of Commerce and the Interior shall, to the extent permitted by law, organize and conduct their monitoring, research, and scientific assessments to support decisionmaking for the Chesapeake Bay ecosystem and to develop the report addressing strengthening environmental monitoring of the Chesapeake Bay and its watershed required in section 202 of this order. This report will assess existing monitoring programs and gaps in data collection, and shall also include the following topics:

    a. the health of fish and wildlife in the Chesapeake Bay watershed;
    b. factors affecting changes in water quality and habitat conditions; and
    c. using adaptive management to plan, monitor, evaluate, and adjust environmental management actions.

Part 9 – Living Resources Protection and Restoration

Sec. 901. The Secretaries of Commerce and the Interior shall, to the extent permitted by law, identify and prioritize critical living resources of the Chesapeake Bay and its watershed, conduct collaborative research and habitat protection activities that address expected outcomes for these species, and develop a report addressing these topics as required in section 202 of this order. The Secretaries of Commerce and the Interior shall coordinate agency activities related to living resources in estuarine waters to ensure maximum benefit to the Chesapeake Bay resources.

Part 10 – Exceptions

Sec. 1001. The heads of agencies may authorize exceptions to this order, in the following circumstances:

    a. during time of war or national emergency;
    b. when necessary for reasons of national security;
    c. during emergencies posing an unacceptable threat to human health or safety or to the marine environment and admitting of no other feasible solution; or
    d. in any case that constitutes a danger to human life or a real threat to vessels, aircraft, platforms, or other man-made structures at sea, such as cases of force majeure caused by stress of weather or other act of God.

Part 11 – General Provisions

Sec. 1101. (a) Nothing in this order shall be construed to impair or otherwise affect:

   i. authority granted by law to a department, agency, or the head thereof; or
   ii. functions of the Director of the Office of Management and Budget relating to budgetary, administrative, or legislative proposals.

(b) This order shall be implemented consistent with applicable law and subject to the availability of appropriations.

(c) This order is not intended to, and does not, create any right or benefit, substantive or procedural, enforceable at law or in equity, by any party against the United States, its departments, agencies, or entities, its officers, employees, or agents, or any other person.

Barack Obama
The White House,
May 12, 2009.

Appendix II

Laws Protecting The Chesapeake Bay and Other Bodies of Water

Statute and Section Purpose

Clcan Water Act:

Sec. 104(n)
Sec. 104(q)
Sec. 201, 202, 204
Sec. 208
Sec. 301
Sec. 301(h)
Sec. 301(k)
Sec. 302
Sec. 303
Sec. 303(e)
Sec. 304
Sec. 304(b)
Sec. 305(b)
Sec: 307
Sec. 308
Sec. 309
Sec. 402

Prohibits, unless authorized by permit, the transportation of wastes for dumping and/or the dumping of wastes into the territorial seas or the contiguous zones.

Authorizes EPA to issue permits for dumping of nondredged materials into the contiguous zone and beyond as long as the materials will not "unreasonably degrade" public health or the marine environment, following criteria specified in statute or established by the Administrator.

167

Authorizes Corps of Engineers to issue permits for dumping dredged material, applying EPA's environmental impact criteria to ensure action will not unreasonably degrade human health or the marine environment.

Specifies permit conditions for waste transported for dumping or to be dumped, issued by EPA or the Coast Guard.

Authorizes EPA and Corps of Engineers to use the resources of other agencies, and instructs the Coast Guard to conduct surveillance and other appropriate enforcement activities as necessary to prevent unlawful transportation of material for dumping or unlawful dumping.

Directs EPA to establish national estuaries programs to prevent and control pollution; to conduct and promote studies of health effects of estuarine pollution.

Establishes a national clearinghouse for the collection and dissemination of information developed on small sewage flows and alternative treatment technologies.

Specifies sewage treatment construction grants program eligibility and Federal share of cost.

Authorizes a process for States and regional agencies to establish comprehensive planning for point and nonpoint source pollution.

Directs States to establish and periodically revise water quality standards for all navigable waters; effluent limitations for point sources requiring BPT should be achieved by July 1, 1977; timetable for achievement of BAT and other standards set. Compliance deadlines for publicly owned treatment works (POTWs) to achieve secondary treatment also set.

Authorizes waivers for POTWs in coastal municipalities from secondary treatment for effluent discharged into marine waters if criteria to protect the marine ecosystem can be met.

Allows industrial dischargers to receive a compliance extension from BAT requirements until July 1, 1987, for installation of an innovative technology, if it will achieve the same or greater effluent reduction than BAT at a significantly lower cost.

Allows EPA to establish additional water quality-based limitations once BAT is established, if necessary to attain or maintain fishable/swimmable water quality (for toxics, the NRDC v. *EPA* consent decree sets terms).

Requires States to adopt and periodically revise water quality standards; if they determine that technology-based standards are not sufficient to meet water quality standards, they must establish total maximum daily loads and waste load allocations, and incorporate more stringent effluent limitations into Sec. 402 permits.

Requires States to establish water quality management plans for watershed basins, to provide for adequate implementation of water quality standards by basin to control nonpoint pollution; Section 208 area wide plans must be consistent with these plans.

Requires EPA to establish and periodically revise water quality criteria to reflect the most recent scientific knowledge about the effects and fate of pollutants, and to maintain the chemical, physical, and biological integrity of navigable waters, groundwater, and ocean waters and establish guidelines for effluent limitations.

Outlines factors to be considered when assessing BPT and BAT to set effluent limitation guidelines, including accounting for "non-water quality impact," age of equipment, etc.

Sets State water quality reporting requirements.

Sets new source performance standards for a list of categories of sources.

Requires EPA to issue categorical pretreatment standards for new and existing indirect sources; POTWs required to adopt and implement local pretreatment programs; toxic effluent limitation standards must be set according to the best available technology economically achievable.

Requires owners or operators of point sources to maintain records and monitoring equipment, do sampling, and provide such information or any additional information.

Gives enforcement powers primarily to State authorities. Civil penalties, however, and misdemeanor sanctions can be issued by EPA in U.S. district courts for violation of the act, including permit conditions or limitations; EPA also is authorized to issue criminal penalties for violations of Sections 301, 302, 306, 307, and 308. EPA may take enforcement action for violations of Section 307(d) which introduce toxic pollutants into POTWs.

Establishes National Pollutant Discharge Elimination System (NPDES), authorizing EPA Administrator to issue a permit for the discharge of any pollutant(s) to navigable waters that will meet requirements of Sections 301, 302, 306, 307 and other relevant sections; States can assume administrative responsibility of the permit program.

Ch. 7—Statutes and Programs Relating To Marine Waste Disposal l 145

Western Atlantic and U.S. Coastal Waters – North Carolina – Sunken Military Craft Act (SMCA) – Prohibition on Disturbing, Removing Artifacts or Damaging Sunken Craft

All mariners are advised of the special protections provided to sunken military craft by the "Sunken Military Craft Act" (SMCA) (Public Law 108- 375). Along the U.S. East Coast, and particularly off North Carolina, there are many sunken U.S. and foreign military craft. Sunken military craft may be the final resting places of military personnel who died in service to their country and are also important historical resources. One very notable example is the wreck of the USS MONITOR, off the NC Coast, also protected by the National Marine Sanctuaries Act. Under international and U.S. law, sunken foreign military craft, including those located in U.S. waters, remain the property of their respective country's government. Sovereign immune vessels, such as military crafts, are afforded protections under U.S. and international law. Included among these vessels are at least three known sunken German submarines (commonly called U-boats) located in waters off the North Carolina coast. These U-boats remain the property of the Federal Republic of Germany. In accordance with the SMCA, no person shall engage in or attempt to engage in any activity directed at a sunken military craft that disturbs, removes, or injures the sunken craft or the associated contents of the craft except as authorized by law. This includes, but is not limited to, the equipment, cargo, contents of the vessel, and the remains and personal effects of the crew and passengers. Mariners are urged to exercise due care when operating in the vicinity of military wrecks, as they can be damaged by both purposeful or inadvertent activities including anchoring, fishing, diving, and other marine activities. Special dangers, such as unexploded ordnance, may also be associated with sunken military craft, and should be considered when operating in these areas. Violations of the SMCA may subject individuals to penalties of up to $100,000 and to liability for damages. Mariners who witness theft of material from, disturbance of, or damage to a sunken military craft are asked to report it to the nearest U.S. Coast Guard unit.[1]

Chesapeake Bay Accords

"The Air Force has agreed to abide by the provisions of the Chesapeake Bay Preservation Act. The purpose of the preservation areas is to protect and improve the water quality of the Chesapeake Bay and its tributaries. These areas consist of Resource Protection Areas and Resource Management Areas. Resource Protection Areas are tidal shores, tidal wetlands, tributary perennial streams, and a 100-foot buffer zone landward of the Resource Protection Area. The Resource Management Area is a 100-foot area landward of the Resource Protection Area that includes floodplains, highly erodible soils including steep slopes, highly permeable soils, and non-tidal wetlands not included in the Resource Protection Area. The purpose of preserving these areas is to prevent increases and to ultimately reduce non-point source pollution into the Chesapeake Bay. General performance criteria have been developed for land inside the Resource Protection Areas including minimizing land disturbance as much as possible, preserving native vegetation, minimizing impervious cover, and other criteria. This is a state program administered by local governments."

A guidance document signed by DoD and EPA, *Management principles for Implementing Response Actions at Closed, Transfering, and Transferred (CTT) Ranges* March 7, 2000 states, "DoD and EPPA are fully committed to the substantive involvement of States and Indian Tribes throughout the response process at CTT ranges. In many cases, a State or Indian Tribe will be the lead regulator at a CTT range."

---

[1]LOCAL NOTICE TO MARINERS, District: 5, Week: 12/10

Misc. Statute Sections

- Rivers and Harbors Act of 1899, section 10
- Clean Water Act of 1972, as amended (33 usc 466), emphasizing sections 115, 313(a), and 404
- Fish and Wildlife Coordination Act of 1958 (16 usc 661 et. Seq.)
- Fish and Wildlife Conservation Act of 1980
- Endangered Species Act of 1973, as amended (16 usc 1531)
- Migratory Bird Act of 1918
- Migratory Bird Treaty Act of 1972 (16 usc 703-711)
- Coastal Zone Management Act of 1972 (16 usc 1451), sec. 307 c3
- National Environmental Policy Act of 1969 (42 usc 4321 et. Seq)
- Executive Order 11990

Appendix III

Military Facilities In The Norfolk, Virginia Area Coast Guard Restrictions Due To Military Operations

(List compiled by John Bull, et al.)

1. Naval Air Station, Norfolk, Va.
2. Joint Operations Center, Norfolk, Va.
3. Base Material Office, NOB, Norfolk, Va.
4. Amphibious Training Base, Norfolk, Va.
5. Naval Operating Base, Norfolk, Va.
6. Cable Censor, Norfolk, Va.
7. Superintending Civil Engineer of Area Number Three, Norfolk, Va.
8. Naval Advisor to Field Office of Division of Contract Distribution, War Production Management, Norfolk, Va.
9. Officer in Charge of Construction of "Civil Works" Contracts, Norfolk Shipbuilding and Dry Dock Co., Norfolk, Va.
10. Naval Net Depot, NOB, Norfolk, Va.
11. Advance Base Section, Naval Supply Depot, Norfolk, Va.
12. Naval Landing Force Equipment Depot, Norfolk, Va.
13. Naval Supply Depot, NOB, Norfolk, Va.
14. Fleet Aviation Disbursing Office, Reports to Senior Naval Aviator, Fleet Air Detachment, Naval Air Station, Naval Operating Base, Norfolk, Va.
15. Branch Hydrographic Office, Norfolk, Va.
16. Supervisory Cost Inspector, 5th ND., Norfolk, Va.
17. Resident Inspector of Naval Material, Texas Co., Petroleum Products, Norfolk, Va.
18. Base Depot, FMF, Norfolk, Va.
19. Marine Barracks, NOB, Norfolk, Va.
20. Navy Recruiting Sub-Station, Norfolk, Va.
21. Naval Drydock, Navy Yard, Norfolk, Va.
22. Fleet Aviation Central Stores Office, Norfolk, Va.
23. Harbor Entrance Control Post, Norfolk, Va.

24. Naval Hospital, NOB, Norfolk, Va.
25. Assistant Industrial Manager, NOB, Norfolk, Va.
26. Inshore Patrol, Norfolk, Va.
27. Navy Cost Inspector, Colona's Shipyard, Incorp., Berkley, Norfolk, Va.
28. Navy Cost Inspector, Craig Brothers Marine Railway, Norfolk, Va.
29. Navy Cost INspector, Moon Shipyard & Repair Corp., Norfolk, Va.
30. Navy Cost Inspector Norfolk Shipbuilding &amnp; Dry Dock Corp., Norfolk, Va.
31. Navy Cost Inspector, Old Dominion Marine Railway Corp., Berkley, Norfolk, Va.
32. Navy Cost Inspector, Thomas Marine Railway, Berkley, Norfolk, Va.
33. Port Director, Norfolk, Va.
34. Inspector of Petroleum Products in Norfolk Area, Norfolk, Va.
35. Public Works Office, NOB, Norfolk, Va.
36. Branch Office of Naval Officer Procurement, Norfolk, Va.
37. Receiving Station, NOB, Norfolk, Va.
38. Sup's Service Store, NAS, Norfolk, Va.
39. Fifth Naval District Permanent Shore Patrol, Norfolk, Va.
40. Naval Training Station, NOB, Norfolk, Va.
41. Advanced Base Aviation Training Unit, NAS, Norfolk, Va.
42. Aviation Free Gunnery Training Unit, NAS, Norfolk, Va.
43. Aircraft Armament Unit, NAS, Norfolk, Va.
44. Transient Officers Training Unit, Service Force, Atlantic (Subordinate Command), NOB, Norfolk, Va.
45. Norfolk Field Office, Norfolk, Va.
46. Standard Landing Craft Unit 3, NOB, Norfolk, Va.
47. Ships' Store Ashore, Camp Bradford, Norfolk, Va.
48. Amphibious Training Case, Camp Bradford, NOB, Norfolk, Va.
49. Fighter Director School, NAS, Norfolk, Va.
50. Naval Training School (Degaussing), NYd, Norfolk, Va.
51. Radar Material School, NOB, Norfolk, Va.
52. Fleet Service Schools (Radar), Virginia Beach, NOB, Norfolk, Va.
53. Captain of the Port, U.S. Coast Guard, Norfolk, Va.
54. U.S. Maritime Service Recruiting Station, Norfolk, Va.
55. Joint Air Amphibious Training School (Reports to Amphibious Training Base, Camp Bradford, NOB, Norfolk, Va.)
56. Marine Barracks, Naval Supply Depot, Norfolk, Va. (Cheatham Annex).
57. Naval Hydrographic Distributing Office, NOB, Norfolk, Va.
58. Navy Relief Office, NOB, Norfolk, Va.
59. First Base Depot, NOB, Norfolk, Va.
60. Base Service Unit, USN, Norfolk, Va.
61. Commander, Training Activities & Rear Echelon, Amphibious Force, Atlantic Fleet, NOB, Norfolk, Va.
62. Maritime Commission Depot, Norfolk.

63. Commander Training Center, Amphibious Training Base, Camp Bradford, NOB, Norfolk, Va.
64. Destroyer Escort School, Naval Training Station, Norfolk, Va.
65. Office of Director of Tugs, NOB, Norfolk, Va.
66. Industry Cooperation Division, Office of Procurement and Material, Norfolk, Va.
67. Amphibious Forces Model Workshop at [CAMP] Bradford, NAS, Norfolk, Va.
68. U.S. Coast Guard District Officer, Norfolk, Va.
69. Joint Air-Amphibious Signal Communications Training School, Camp Bradford, NOB, Norfolk, Va.
70. Amphibious Communication School, NOB, Norfolk, Va.
71. Joint Communication School, Amphibious Training Base, Little Creek, Va.
72. Fleet Service Schools, NOB, Norfolk, Va.
73. Physical Instructors School, Naval Training Station, NOB, Norfolk, Va.
74. Naval Training School (Torpedomen), NTS, Norfolk, Va.
75. Recruiting Training School, NTS, NOB, Norfolk, Va.
76. Beach Party School, Norfolk, Va.
77. Naval Training School (Fire Controlmen), NTS, Norfolk, Va.
78. Fire Fighters School, NOB, Norfolk, Va.
79. Destroyer Escort Assembly & Training Center, NTS, Norfolk, Va.
80. Fire Damage Control School, NOB, Norfolk, Va.
81. Registered Publications Issuing Office, NOB, Norfolk, Va.
82. Degaussing Office, NOB, Norfolk, Va.
83. Epidemiological Unit 24, NOB, Norfolk, Va.
84. Naval Fuel Depot, NOB, Norfolk, Va.
85. Norfolk Fighter Wing, 1st Fighter Command, Norfolk Army Activity.
86. Navy Market Office, Quartermaster Market Center, Norfolk, Va.
87. Classification Center NOB, Norfolk, Va.
88. U.S. Navy Accounting, 5th ND., Norfolk, Va.
89. Pre-Commissioning Training Center, NTS, NOB, Norfolk, Va.
90. Resident Office in Charge of Construction Contract NOy-6943.
91. Accounting Department, NOB, Norfolk.
92. Educational Services Program, Receiving Station, Norfolk, Va.
93. District Intelligence Office, NOB, Norfolk, Va.
94. Fire Prevention Inspection Board, Service Force Atlantic Fleet, Subordinate Command, NOV, Norfolk, Va.
95. Navy V-12 Training School, Naval Receiving Station, Norfolk, Va.
96. Public Works Indoctrination School, NOB, Norfolk, Va.
97. Commissary Store, NOB, Norfolk, Va.

98. Branch of Material Redistribution and Disposal Section, Stock Division, Bureau of Supplies and Account, Norfolk, Va.
99. U.S. Naval Barracks, NOB, Norfolk, Va.
100. District Air Office, 5th ND.
101. District Ordnance Office, NOB, Norfolk, Va.
102. Chaplain's Department, NOB, Norfolk, Va.
103. Naval Advisor, War Production Board, Norfolk, Va.
104. War Bond Office, Norfolk, Va.
105. District Civilian Personnel Office, Norfolk, Va.
106. District Disbursing Office, Norfolk, Va.
107. District Inspection Office, 5th ND.
108. Fleet Air Detachment, NAS, Norfolk.
109. District Liaison Office, 5th ND.
110. Base Material Office, 5th ND.
111. Office of Director of Personnel, Norfolk, Va.
112. Police Office, Norfolk, Va.
113. Public Relations Office, Norfolk, Va.
114. District Recreation & Physical Training Department, Norfolk, Va.
115. Material Redistribution & Disposal Office, Norfolk.
116. Dental Prosthetic Facility, NOB, Norfolk, Va.
117. Director of Training, NOB, Norfolk, Va.
118. Traffic and Transportation Office, NOB, Norfolk, Va.
119. Water Transportation Service, NOB, Norfolk, Va.
120. District Supply Office, Norfolk, Va.
121. Aviation Repair Unit #2, NAS, Norfolk, Va.
122. District War Plans, Hdqts., Norfolk, Va.
123. [NAVAL] Armed Guard School, Selton, Norfolk, Va.
124. Naval Fuel Annex, Craney Island, Norfolk, Va.
125. Joint Air Amphibious Signal Communication School, Amphibious Training Base, Camp Bradford, NOB, Norfolk, Va.
126. Anti-Submarine Warfare School, NTS, NOB, Norfolk, Va.
127. Camp Bradford, NOB, Norfolk, Va.
128. Joint Communications School, Amphibious Training Base, Camp Bradford, NOB, Norfolk, Va.
129. OinC of Construction of Civil Works Contracts, Norfolk Shipbuilding and Drydock Co., at Tidewater Construction Co., Berkley Station, Norfolk.
130. Bureau of Ships Field Representative for Ship Repair Unit, 5th ND.
131. Barrage Balloon School, Amphibious Training Base, Camp Bradford, NOB, Norfolk, Va.
132. District Classification Control Officer, 5th ND.
133. Link Celestial Navigation Training Unit, NAS, Norfolk, Va.
134. Naval Training School (Diesel Advanced), NTS, NOB, Norfolk, Va.
135. Naval Medical Supply Storehouse, NOB, Norfolk, Va.
136. Night Lookout Training Units, NTS, NOB, Norfolk, Va.

137. Naval Training School (Welders), NTS, NOB, Norfolk, Va.
138. Labor Board, NOB, Norfolk, Va.
139. Position Classification Field Office, Norfolk, Va.
140. Aviation Supply Depot, Norfolk, Va.
141. Degaussing Range (Sewall Point), Norfolk, Va.
142. Deperming Station (Lambert Point), Norfolk, Va.
143. Naval Barracks, Naval Supply Depot, Norfolk, Va.
144. Atlantic Fleet Weather Central, Norfolk, Va.
145. Naval Radio Station, NOB, Norfolk, Va.
146. Degaussing Range (Wolf Trap), Norfolk, Va.
147. District Civil Readjustment Office, Norfolk, Va.
148. Fleet Post Office, NOB, Norfolk, Va.
149. Fleet Service Schools (Machinists Mates), NOB, Norfolk, Va.
150. Fire Fighters School, Amphibious Training Base, Camp Bradford, NOB,   Norfolk, Va.
151. Domestic Transportation Office, 5th ND., Norfolk, Va.
152. District Property Transportation Officer, 5th ND., Norfolk, Va.
153. Advanced Base Supply Training Unit (Norfolk Detachment), NAS, Norfolk, Va.
154. Family Clinic, Merrimack Park, NOB, Norfolk, Va.
155. Bureau of Aeronautics Maintenance Representative Office, Eastern District, NAS, Norfolk, Va.
156. Training Aids Section, NOB, Norfolk, Va.
157. District Benefits and Insurance Office, Norfolk, Va.
158. Wartime Merchant Ship Communication School, Norfolk, Va.
159. Navy Reservation Bureau, Norfolk, Va.
160. Naval Training School (Laundry), Armed Guard School, Shelton, Norfolk, Va.
161. Naval Training School (Refrigeration), NTS, NOB, Norfolk, Va.
162. Combat Aircrew Training Unit, NAS, Norfolk, Va.
163. U.S. Naval Disciplinary Barracks, NOB, Norfolk, Va.
164. Air Support Training Unit #6, NAS, Norfolk, Va.
165. Civil Works Engineer, Norfolk Civil Works District, Norfolk, Va.
166. LSM Loading and Servicing Detail, Imperial Docks, Norfolk, Va.
167. Navy Accounts Disbursing Office, NOB, Norfolk, Va.
168. Research and Development Center, Fleet Operational Training Command, Atlantic Fleet, NOB, Norfolk, Va.
169. Electronic Maintenance Training Unit, Air Force, Atlantic Fleet, NAS, Norfolk, Va. (Info only).

Appendix IV

Listing of Related Defense and Chesapeake Bay Research

Consult the website:
www.stormingmedia.us/keywords/chesapeake_bay.html

Appendix V

Title 33 – Navigation And Navigable Waters

CHAPTER II – Corps of Engineers, Department of the Army, Department of Defense Part 334–Danger Zone and Restricted Area Regulations

CFR Data is current as of August 23, 2012

§334.240	Potomac River, Mattawoman Creek and Chicamuxen Creek; U.S. Naval Surface Weapons Center, Indian Head Division, Indian Head, Md.
§334.250	Gunston Cove, at Whitestone Point, Va.; U.S. Army restricted area.
§334.260	York River, Va.; naval restricted areas.
§334.270	York River adjacent to Cheatham Annex Depot, Naval Supply Center, Williamsburg, Va.; restricted area.
§334.275	North and Southwest Branch, Back River, Hampton, U.S. Air Force Base, Langley, Va.; restricted area.
§334.280	James River between the entrance to Skiffes Creek and Mulberry Point, Va.; army training and small craft testing area.
§334.290	Elizabeth River, Southern Branch, Va., naval restricted areas.
§334.293	Elizabeth River, Craney Island Refueling Pier Restricted Area, Portsmouth VA; naval restricted area.
§334.300	Hampton Roads and Willoughby Bay, Norfolk Naval Base, naval restricted area, Norfolk, Virginia.
§334.310	Chesapeake Bay, Lynnhaven Roads; navy amphibious training area.
§334.320	Chesapeake Bay entrance; naval restricted area.
§334.330	Atlantic Ocean and connecting waters in vicinity of Myrtle Island, Va.; Air Force practice bombing, rocket firing, and gunnery range.
§334.340	Chesapeake Bay off Plumtree Island, Hampton, Va.; Air Force precision test area.
§334.350	Chesapeake Bay off Fort Monroe, Va.; firing range danger zone.
§334.360	Chesapeake Bay off Fort Monroe, Virginia; restricted area, U.S. Naval Base and Naval Surface Weapon Center.
§334.370	Chesapeake Bay, Lynnhaven Roads; danger zones, U.S. Naval Amphibious Base.
§334.380	Atlantic Ocean south of entrance to Chesapeake Bay off Dam Neck, Virginia; naval firing range.
§334.390	Atlantic Ocean south of entrance to Chesapeake Bay; firing range.
§334.400	Atlantic Ocean south of entrance to Chesapeake Bay off Camp Pendleton, Virginia; naval restricted area.

Appendix VI

Federal Facilities Superfund Sites

Chesapeake Bay

Site Name	EPA ID	NPL Status	City	County	Zip	State
Aberdeen Proving Ground - Edgewood Area	MD2210020036	Final	Aberdeen	Harford	21001	MD
Aberdeen Proving Ground - Michaelsville LF	MD3210021355	Final	Aberdeen	Harford	21005	MD
Allegany Ballistics Lab	WV0170023691	Final	Short Gap	Mineral	26753	WV
Andrews Air Force Base	MD0570024000	Final	Andrews AFB	Prince Georges	20331	MD
Beltsville Agricultural Research Center (USDA)	MD0120508940	Final	Beltsville	Prince Georges	20705	MD
Brandywine DRMO	MD9570024803	Final	Andrews	Prince Georges	20331	MD
Camp Simms		Non	Washington	DC	20032	DC
Curtis Bay Coast Guard Yard	MD4690307844	Final	Baltimore	Anne Arundel	21226	MD
Defense Supply Center Philadelphia	PA09715900005	Non	Philadelphia	Philadelphia	19101	PA
Defense General Supply Center	VA3971520751	Final	Richmond	Chesterfield	23297	VA
Dover AF Base	DE8570024010	Final	Dover	Kent	19901	DE
Former Nansemond Ordnance Depot	VAD123933426	Final	Suffolk	Suffolk	23434	VA
Fort Eustis	VA6210020321	Final	Newport News	Newport News	23604	VA
Ft. Detrick Area B Groundwater	MDD985397249	Final	Frederick	Frederick		MD

Site Name	EPA ID	NPL Status	City	County	Zip	State
Ft. George G. Meade	MD9210020567	Final	Odenton	Anne Arundel	20755	MD
Fort Pickett	VA2210020705	Non	Blackstone	Nottoway	23824	VA
Ft. Ritchie	MD0000795211	Non	Cascade	Washington	21719	MD
Indian Head Naval Surface Warfare Center	MD7170024684	Final	Indian Head	Charles	20640	MD
Langley AFB/NASA Research Cntr	VA2800005033	Final	Hampton	Hampton	23665	VA
Letterkenny Army Depot PDO Area	PA2210090054	Final	Chambersburg	Franklin	17201	PA
Letterkenny Army Depot SE Area	PA6213820503	Final	Chambersburg	Franklin	17201	PA
Marine Corps Combat Development Comand	VA1170024722	Final	Quantico	Prince William	22134	VA
Middletown Air Field	PAD980538763	Deleted	Middletown	Dauphin	17057	PA
NASA Wallops Island	VA8800010763	Non	Wallops Island	Accomack	23337	VA
Naval Air Development Cntr	PA6170024545	Final	Warminster	Bucks	18974	PA
Naval Amphibious Base	VA5170022482	Final	Norfolk	Virginia Beach	23521	VA
Naval Support Station	PA3170022104	Non	Mechanicsburg	Cumberland	17055	PA
Naval Surface Warfare Center	VA7170024684	Final	Dahlgren	King George	22448	VA
Naval Surface Warfare Center - White Oak	MD0170023444	Non	Silver Spring	Montgomery	20903	MD
Naval Training Center Bainbridge	MDD985397256	Non	Bainbridge	Cecil	21904	MD
Naval Weapons Station Yorktown	VA8170024170	Final	Yorktown	York	23690	VA
Naval Weapons Station Yorktown - Cheatham Annex	VA3170024605	Final	Williamsburg	Williamsburg	23185	VA
Norfolk Naval Base	VA6170061463	Final	Norfolk	Norfolk	23511	VA
Norfolk Naval Shipyard	VA1170024813	Final	Portsmouth	Portsmouth	23709	VA
Patuxent River Naval Air Station	MD7170024536	Final	Patuxent River	St Marys	20670	MD
Philadelphia Naval Complex	PA4170022418	Non	Philadelphia	Philadelphia	19112	PA
St. Elizabeth's Hospital		Non	Washington	DC	20032	DC
St Julien's Creek Annex (US Navy)	VA5170000181	Final	Chesapeake	Chesapeake	23702	VA
Southeast Federal Center		Non	Washington	DC	20408	DC

Site Name	EPA ID	NPL Status	City	County	Zip	State
Tobyhanna Army Depot	PA5213820892	Final	Tobyhanna	Monroe	18466	PA
USA Cameron Station	VA4210220139	Non	Alexandria	Alexandria	22304	VA
USA Radford Ammuntion Plant	VA1210020730	Non	Radford	Radford City	24141	VA
USA Support Oakdale formerly: C.E. Kelly Support Facility	PA5210022344	Non	Oakdale	Allegheny	15071	PA
USN NRTF-Driver	VA9170022488	Non	Suffolk	Suffolk	23434	VA
Valley Forge National Historic Park	PA9141733080	Non	Valley Forge	Chester	19481	PA
Vint Hill Farms Station	VA8210020931	Non	Warrenton	Fauquier	22186	VA
Warrenton Training Center	VAD988189312	Non	Warrenton	Fauquier	22186	VA
Washington DC Chemical Munitions (Spring Valley)	DCD983971136	Non	Washington	DC	20015	DC
Washington Gas & Light		Non	Washington	DC	20019	DC
Washington National Airport	VAD988166518	Non	Arlington	Arlington	22030	VA
Washington Navy Yard	DC9170024310	Final	Washington	DC	20374	DC
West Virginia Ordnance	WVD980713036	Final	Pt Pleasant	Mason	25550	WV
Willow Grove Naval Air Station	PAD987277837	Final	Willow Grove	Montgomery	19090	PA
Woodbridge Research Facility (WRF)	VA7210020981	Non	Woodbridge	Prince William	22191	VA

Appendix VII

1994 Tri Data

The 1994 TRI data were the first to reflect releases from federal facilities. The Bay Watershed's 25 federal facilities reported releases and transfers of 834,529 pounds of TRI chemicals in 1994.

That included:

- 167,635 pounds from five facilities in the District of Columbia
- 205,019 pounds from nine facilities in Maryland
- 10,400 pounds from one facility in New York
- 372,597 pounds from seven facilities in Virginia

There were no federal facilities in the Bay watershed portions of West Virginia and Delaware that were required to report.

The facilities with the largest TRI releases included:

- U.S. Navy Norfolk Naval Base, Norfolk, Va. – 107,105 pounds
- U.S. Navy Norfolk Naval Shipyard, Portsmouth, Va. – 100,020 pounds
- U.S. Department of Agriculture Beltsville Agricultural Research Center, Beltsville, Md. –79,820 pounds
- U.S. Army Letterkenny Army Depot, Chambersburg, Pa. – 65,107 pounds
- NASA Langley Research Center, Hampton, Va. – 32,000 pounds

Nationwide, 191 federal facilities reported releases of more than 9.8 million pounds of TRI chemicals in 1994.

Federal facilities were exempt from the law until an executive order issued by President Clinton in August 1993 required them to begin filing reports. In addition, the executive order also directed each federal agency to reduce releases and off-site transfers of toxic chemicals by 50 percent by 1999 using the 1994 numbers as a baseline.

Appendix VIII

Installations Within The Chesapeake Bay Watershed

Air Force

Andrews Air Force Base
Bolling Air Force Base
    Brandywine Global Communications
        Receiving Station
Davidsonville Communications Station
Langley Air Force Base

Army

Aberdeen Proving Ground
Adelphi Laboratory Center
Blossom Point Research Facility
Carlisle Barracks
Fort A.P. Hill
Fort Belvoir
Fort Detrick
Fort Eustis
Fort Indiantown Gap
Fort Lee
Fort McNair
Fort Meade
Fort Monroe
Fort Myer
Fort Story
Letterkenny Army Depot
Scranton Army Ammunition Plant
Walter Reed Army Medical Center
Warrenton Training Center

Army Corps of Engineers

Almond Lake
Alvin R. Bush Dam
Arkport Dam
Aylesworth Lake
Cowanesque Lake
Craney Island Dredge Spoils Disposal Area
Curwensville Lake
East Sidney Lake
Foster J. Sayers Dam
Hammond Lake
Indian Rock Dam
Jennings Randolph Lake
Lake Moomaw
Raystown Lake
Savage River Dam
Stillwater Lake
Tioga Lake
Whitney Point Lake

Defense Logistics Agency

Defense Distribution Depot Susquehanna
Defense Supply Center, Richmond

Department of Defense

Arlington National Cemetery
Pentagon

Marine Corps

Henderson Hall
Marine Barracks, Washington
Marine Corps Base Quantico

Navy

Allegheny Ballistics Laboratory
Armed Forces Experimental Training Activity
    Camp Peary
Defense Fuel Supply Point Craney Island

National Naval Medical Center Bethesda
Naval Air Station Oceana
Naval Amphibious Base Little Creek
Naval Medical Center Portsmouth
Naval Station Norfolk
Naval Station Norfolk, Lafayette River Annex
Naval Station Norfolk, St. Helena Annex
Naval Station Norfolk, St. Juliens Creek Annex
Naval Support Activity Mechanicsburg
Naval Support Facility Anacostia
Naval Support Facility Andrews
Naval Support Facility Annapolis
Naval Support Facility Arlington
Naval Support Facility Carderock
Naval Support Facility Chesapeake Beach
Naval Support Facility Dahlgren
Naval Support Facility Indian Head
Naval Support Facility Naval Research Laboratory
Naval Support Facility Patuxent River
Naval Support Facility Patuxent River,
    Bloodsworth Island
Naval Support Facility Potomac Annex
Naval Support Facility Solomons Island
Naval Support Facility Suitland
Naval Support Facility Thurmont
Naval Weapons Station Yorktown
Naval Weapons Station Yorktown,
Cheatham Annex
Naval Weapons Station Yorktown Fuels
OLF Webster Field
Navy Information Operations Command, Sugar Grove
Norfolk Naval Shipyard
U.S. Naval Academy
U.S. Naval Academy Dairy Farm
U.S. Naval Support Facility Observatory
Washington Navy Yard

Appendix IX

Fish Advisories

Table 1b Fish advisories for Virginia waters near the District of Columbia.

Species	Water body	Recommended meals per month	Contaminant (Risk driver)
American eel	Tributaries between MD/VA line near Route 340 Bridge and I-395 Bridge	No more than two	PCBs
American eel Bullhead catfish Channel catfish (<18″) Gizzard shad 　Largemouth bass 　Smallmouth bass 　Sunfish Striped bass 　White catfish White 　perch Yellow perch	Tributaries and embayments between I-395 Bridge and Route 301 Bridge	No more than two	PCBs
Carp Channel catfish (>18″)	Tributaries and embayments between I-395 Bridge and Route 301 Bridge	Do not eat	PCBs

High risk individuals such as women who are pregnant or may become pregnant, nursing mothers, and young children are advised not to eat any fish contaminated either with polychlorinated biphenyls (PCBs) or mercury from the respective advisory areas.

From: **Analysis of Contaminant Concentrations in Fish Tissue Collected from the Waters of the District of Columbia,** Publication No. CBFO-C08-03 Alfred E. Pinkney, U.S. Fish and Wildlife Service Chesapeake Bay Field Office, March, 2009.

Fish advisories for Maryland Waters Near the District of Columbia

Recommended number of meals per year					
Species	Water body	General population (8-ounce meal)	Women (6-ounce meal)	Children (3-ounce meal)	Contaminant (Risk driver)
American eel	Anacostia [a]	15	11	8	PCBs
	Potomac [b]	19	15	11	PCBs
Brown bullhead	Anacostia	9	7	avoid	PCBs
Channel catfish	Anacostia	9	7	avoid	PCBs
	Potomac (<18″)	8	6	avoid	PCBs
	Potomac (>18″)	7	avoid	avoid	PCBs
Carp	Potomac	11	8	6	PCBs
Striped bass	Ches Bay tributaries: <28″ May 16–Dec 15	25	19		PCBs
	Ches Bay tributaries: >28″ April 15				PCBs
Sunfish	Anacostia River	35	27	21	PCBs
Small and largemouth bass	Statewide default	48	48	24	Methylmercury
White catfish	Potomac (<18″)	17	13	10	PCBs
	Potomac (.18″)	12	avoid	avoid	PCBs

[a]Advisories for the Anacostia River are for the main stem and tributaries below MD Route 193

[b]Advisories for the Potomac River from the DC line downriver to the MD 301 Bridge

Bibliography

1. Ocean Dumping (Including Munitions) Books and Articles

Advisory Committee on Protection of the Sea (ACOPS), Coastal Survey of Packaged Chemical and other Hazardous Items 2002/2003, Maritime and Coastguard Agency Research Project No. 488, London, October 2003.

Agriculture and Fisheries Dept for Scotland, ICI Nobels Explosives Company Ltd: Disposal of Waste Materials arising from the Production of Explosives, Department of Agriculture and Fisheries for Scotland, 1990.

Albright, RD, *Cleanup of Chemical and Explosive Munitions*, 2nd Edition, Elsevier 2012.

Andersson, A-C, Eriksson, J, Nygren, Y, Hagglund, L and Forsman, M, Risk-Assessment of Dumped Ammunition in Aquatic Environment, Abstract, PB2000-101476, ISSN 1104-9154, Defence Research Establishment, Sweden, December 1998.

Andersson, A-C, Eriksson, J, Hagglund, L, Nygren Y, Johansson, T and Forsman, M, Simulation of TNT Leakage in Sea Environment, Abstract, PB2003-100496, ISSN 1650-1942, Swedish Defence Research Agency, December 2001.

Andrulewicz, E, War gases and ammunition in the Polish economic zone of the Baltic Sea, in *Sea-Dumped Chemical Weapons: Aspects, Problems and Solutions*, Ed. AV Kaffka, Kluwer Academic Publishers, Dordrecht, 1996, pp 9–15.

Anon., Mustard gas in the Baltic Sea, *Marine Pollution Bulletin*, 1969, pp 17–18.

Anon., World War II poisons, *Marine Pollution Bulletin*, 7, 1976, p 179.

Anon., An account of the environmental, health and security situation in connection with the dumped poison gas ammunition in the waters surrounding Denmark, Miljøstyrelsen, Copenhagen, 1985.

Anon., "VI Military Defence" from the Coastal Guide organisation web-site, http://www.coastalguide.org/code/defmili.html, updated 13th November 1999.

Anon., Dumped munitions resurface, News, *Marine Pollution Bulletin*, No.12, December 1995, p 768.

Batten, JJ, Moore, BT and Smith BS, Marine corrosion: Case histories in failure analysis from defence, Proceedings of the 30th Annual Conference: CASS 90: corrosion - air, sea, soil, Paper 16, Australasian Corrosion Association Inc. Conference, Auckland, New Zealand, November 1990.

Beddington, J. FRS and A.J. Kinloch, FREng., *Munitions Dumped at Sea: A Literature Review*, IC Consultants Ltd, London, June 2005

Belden, JB, Ownby, DR, Lotufo, GR, and Lydy, MJ, Accumulation of Trinitrotoluene (TNT) in aquatic organisms: Part 2 - Bioconcentration in aquatic invertebrates and potential for trophic transfer to channel catfish (Ictalurus punctatus), *Chemosphere*, 2005, pp 1161–1168.

Berglind, R and Liljedahl, B, Compounds in dumped and unexploded ordnance – Possible environmental hazards, Abstract, PB2000-101463, ISSN 1104-9154, Defence Research Establishment Sweden, October 1998.

BBC News Online UK, Mines and hand grenades washed ashore, http://news. bbc.co.uk/1/low/uk/1536893.stm,11th September 2001.

BBC News Web-site, Alex Kirby, UK's undersea "ticking time-bombs", http:// news.bbc.co.uk/1/hi/sci/tech/4032629.stm, 26th November 2004.

Bowles, R, Press Brief by MoD – re: Allegations in Scottish press on sea dumping of chemical weapons (CW), D News Pol 2, D/D SEF Pol/4/9/3, March 2002.

Brannon, JM, Price, CB, Yost, SL, Hayes, C and Porter, B, Comparison of environmental fate and transport process descriptors of explosives in saline and freshwater systems, *Marine Pollution Bulletin*, 2005, pp 247–251.

British Geological Survey, Analysis of explosions in the BGS seismic database in the area of Beaufort's Dyke, 1992–2004', CR/05/064, 2005.

Carr, RS, Nipper, M, Biedenbach, JM, Hooten, RL, Miller, K and Saepoff, S, Sediment toxicity identification evaluation (TIE) studies at marine sites suspected of ordnance contamination, *Archives of Environmental Contamination and Toxicology*, No.3, October 2001, pp 298–307.

Carter LJ, Nerve gas disposal: How the AEC refused to take Army off the hook, *Science*, New series, No. 3952, 25th September 1970, pp 1296–1298.

CHEMU, Complex analysis of the hazard related to the captured German chemical weapon dumped in the Baltic Sea, CHEMU 2/2/1/Rev.1 (27 September 1993): as amended 11 October 1993 - submitted by Russia.

Chepesiuk, R, A sea of trouble?, *The Bulletin of the Atomic Scientists*, No. 5, September/October 1997, pp 40–44.

Clark, RB, Frid, C and Attrill, M, *Marine Pollution* (Fourth Edition), Clarendon Press, Oxford, 1997, ISBN 0 19 850069 6, pp 122–124 and pp. 152–155.

Courtney-Green, PR, Options for the demilitarization of explosive ordnance, MSc Thesis, Royal Military College of Science, Shrivenham, November 1990.

Cumming, AS and Paul, NC, Environmental issues of energetic materials: A U.K. perspective, *Waste Management*, No. 2/3, 1997, pp 129–133.

Davenport, R, Johnson, LR, Schaeffer, DJ and Balbach, H, Phototoxicology: 1. Light-enhanced toxicity of TNT and some related compounds to Daphnia magna and Lytechinus variagatus embryos, *Ecotoxicology and Environmental Safety*, 27, 1994, pp 14–22.

Davies, G, Munitions dump explodes into headlines again, News, *Marine Pollution Bulletin*, No. 3, March 1996, pp 250–251.

Dixon, TR, Coastal survey of packaged chemical and other hazardous items, PECD Reference Number 7/8/188. Submitted to CUE Marine Division, Department of the Environment. Advisory Committee on Protection of the Sea. 1992.

Dixon, TR and Dixon, TJ, Munitions in British coastal waters, *Marine Pollution Bulletin*, 1979, pp 352 – 357.

Dixon, TR and Dixon, TJ, A report on a survey of packaged dangerous goods, munitions and pyrotechnics recovered on the beaches and in the nearshore waters of the British Isles (1 September 1982-31 August 1983). Stage 6. Marine Litter Research Programme, Advisory Committee on Protection of the Sea/ Keep Britain Tidy Group, 1985.

Doyle, A, Reuters News Service Report, January 2004.

Duursma, EK (Ed.), *Dumped Chemical Weapons in the Sea – Options*, Published under the auspices of the Dr. A.H. Heineken Foundations for the Environment, 2e Weteringplantsoen 5, 1017 ZD Amsterdam, Netherlands, 1999, ISBN: 90-9012717-8, June 1999.

Duursma, EK and Surikov, BT, in *Dumped Chemical Weapons in the Sea – Options*, Ed. EK. Duursma. Published under the auspices of the Dr.A.H.Heineken Foundations for the Environment, 2e Weteringplantsoen 5, 1017 ZD Amsterdam, Netherlands, 1999, ISBN: 90-9012717-8, June 1999.

Ek, H, Dave, G, Sturve, J, Almroth, BC, Stephensen, E, Forlin, L, and Birgersson, G, Tentative biomarkers for 2,4,6-trinitrotoluene (TNT) in fish (Oncorhynchus mykiss), *Aquatic Toxicology* 72, 2005, pp 221–230.

Edwards, R, Danger from the deep, *New Scientist*, 18th November 1995, pp 16–17.

Ek, H, Dave, G, Birgersson, G and Forlin, L, Acute effects of 2,4,6-trinitrotoluene (TNT) on haematology parameters and hepatic EROD-activity in rainbow trout (Oncorhynchus Mykiss), *Aquatic Ecosystem Health & Management*, 2003, pp 415–421.

Farrington, JW, Davis, AC, Tripp, BW, Phelps, DK and Galloway, WB, "Mussel watch" – Measurements of chemical pollutants in bivalves as one indicator of coastal environmental quality, *New Approaches to Monitoring Aquatic Ecosystems, ASTM STP 940*, Ed. TP Boyle, American Society for Testing and Materials, Philadelphia, 1987, pp 125–139.

Fedorov, LA, Pre-convention liquidation of Soviet chemical weapons, in *Sea-Dumped Chemical Weapons: Aspects, Problems and Solutions*, Ed. AV Kaffka, Kluwer Academic Publishers, Dordrecht, 1996, pp 17–27.

Fisheries Research Services Report (FRSR) No. 15/96, Marine Laboratory, Aberdeen. Surveys of the Beaufort's Dyke explosives disposal site, November 1995-July 1996, Final Report, November 1996.

Fisheries Research Services, Case study: Munitions dumping at Beaufort's Dyke, htttp://www.frs-scotland.gov.uk, 8th April 2004.

Fokin, AV and Babievsky, KK, Chemical "echo" of the wars, in *Sea-Dumped Chemical Weapons: Aspects, Problems and Solutions*, Ed. AV Kaffka, Kluwer Academic Publishers, Dordrecht, 1996, pp 29–33.

Fonnum, F, Investigation of the ships filled with chemical munitions which were sunk off the Norwegian coast after World War II, in *The Challenge of Old Chemical Munitions and Toxic Armament Wastes*, Ed. T Stock, and K Lohs, Sipri Chemical & Biological Warfare Studies, Volume 16, Stockholm International Peace Research Institute/Oxford University Press, 1997, pp 279–290.

Frondorf, MJ, Special study on the sea disposal of chemical munitions by the United States, in *Sea-Dumped Chemical Weapons: Aspects, Problems and Solutions*, Ed. AV Kaffka, Kluwer Academic Publishers, Dordrecht, 1996, pp 35–40.

Glasby, GP, Disposal of chemical weapons in the Baltic Sea, in *The Science of the Total Environment*, 997, pp 267–273.

Granbom PO, Investigation of a dumping area in the Skagerrak, 1992, in *Sea-Dumped Chemical Weapons: Aspects, Problems and Solutions*, Ed. AV Kaffka, Kluwer Academic Publishers, Dordrecht, 1996, pp 41–48.

Green, A, Moore, D and Farrar, D, Chronic toxicity of 2, 4, 6-trinitrotoluene to a marine polychaete and an estuarine amphipod, *Environmental Toxicology and Chemistry*, 1999, pp 1783–1790.

Haas, R, Tsivunchyk, O, Steinbach, K, Low, Ev, Scheibner, K and Hofrichter, M, Conversion of adamsite (phenarsarzin chloride) by fungal manganese peroxidase, *Appl. Microbiol. Biotechnol.*, 63, October 2003, pp 564–566.

Haber, R, and Hedtmann, J, Unexploded ordnance devices: Detection, recovery and disposal, in *Sea-Dumped Chemical Weapons: Aspects, Problems and Solutions*, Ed. AV Kaffka, Kluwer Academic Publishers, Dordrecht, 1996, pp 73–86.

Hansard,15 November 1995.

Hansard, Munitions Dumping (South-west Scotland), 22 November 1995.

Hansard, Beaufort's Dyke, 28 November 1996.

Hansard, Beaufort Trench (Mustard Gas), 23 April 2002

Harrison, P, Where the real nasties lurk, *Diver*, May 1998.

Hart, J, A review of sea-dumped chemical weapons, presented at The Environment and the Common Fisheries Policy, Threats to and Constraints on Sustainability, (Greenwich Forum), The Royal Society, 27 January 2000.

Heintze, H-J, Legal problems related to old chemical munitions dumped in the Baltic Sea, *The Challenge of Old Chemical Munitions and Toxic Armament Wastes*, Sipri Chemical & Biological Warfare Studies, Volume 16, Ed. T Stock and K Lohs, Oxford University Press, 1997, pp 255–290.

HELCOM CHEMU, Report on sea dumping of chemical weapons by the United Kingdom in the Skaggerrak waters post World War Two. Ad Hoc Group on Dumped Chemical Munitions, 2nd Meeting, Vilnius, Lithuania, September 1993.

HELCOM, Vessels sunk in Skagerrak as part of UK CW disposals, Appendix 1 in: Baltic Marine Environment Protection Commission, Helsinki Commission, UK, Report on sea dumping of chemical weapons by the United Kingdom in the Skagerrak waters post World War II, HELCOM CHEMU 2/2/5, 28th September 1993.

HELCOM, Report on chemical munitions dumped in the Baltic Sea, Report to the 16th Meeting of the Helsinki Commission 8–11th March 1994 from the Ad Hoc Working Group on Dumped Chemical Munitions, HELCOM CHEMU, January 1994.

HELCOM, Final report of the ad hoc working group on dumped chemical munition, HELCOM CHEMU to the 16th Meeting of the Helsinki Commission.

HELCOM, Third periodic assessment of the state of the marine environment of the Baltic Sea area 1989–1993, Executive Summary, 1996, *Baltic Sea Environment Proceedings*, No. 64A.

HELCOM, Special problems: Dumping of chemical munition 1996, *Baltic Sea Environment Proceedings*, No. 64B, Chapter 8 pp 198–202.

HELCOM, Environment of the Baltic Sea area 1994–1998, *Baltic Sea Environment Proceedings*, No. 82A, 2001, p13.

HELCOM, Environment of the Baltic Sea area 1994–1998, *Baltic Sea Environment Proceedings*, No. 82A, Chapter 8, 2002, pp 149–152 and 182–184.

HELCOM, Environment of the Baltic Sea area 1999–2002, *Baltic Sea Environment Proceedings*, No. 87, 2003, p 35.

HELCOM, 25 incidents of chemical munitions caught by fisherman in the Baltic Sea reported in 2003, Baltic Marine Environmental Protection Commission of HELCOM, 14th September 2004.

HMSO, *Text Book of Ammunition*, The Naval & Military Press Ltd, ISBN 1843425610, 1936.

Hoffsommer, JC and Rosen, JM, Analysis of explosives in sea water, *Bulletin of Environmental Contamination & Toxicology*, No. 2/3, 1972, pp 177–181.

Irion, G, Schwermetallbelastung in Oberflächensedimenten der westlichen Ostsee, *Natur wissenschaften*, 71, 1984, pp 536 –538.

Kaffka, AV (Ed.), *Sea-Dumped Chemical Weapons: Aspects, Problems and Solutions*, Kluwer Academic Publishers, Dordrecht, ISBN 0-7923-4090-61996, January 1995.

Knightley, P, Dumps of death, *Sunday Times Magazine*, 5th April 1992.

Konkov, VN, The technological problems with sea-dumped chemical weapons from the standpoint of defence conversion industries, in *Sea-Dumped Chemical Weapons: Aspects, Problems and Solutions*, Ed. AV Kaffka, Kluwer Academic Publishers, Dordrecht, 1996, pp 87–91.

Korotenko, KA, Chemical warfare munitions dumped in the Baltic Sea: Modeling of pollutant transport due to possible leakage, *Oceanology*, No. 1, 2003, pp 21–34.

Laurin, F, The Baltic and North Sea dumping of chemical weapons: Still a threat?, in *The Challenge of Old Chemical Munitions and Toxic Armament Wastes*, Ed. Stock, T and Lohs, K, Sipri Chemical & Biological Warfare Studies, Volume 16, Stockholm International Peace Research Institute/Oxford University Press, 1997, pp 263–278.

Leewis, RJ, Environmental impact of shipwrecks in the North Sea. II. Negative aspects: Hazardous substances in shipwrecks, *Wat. Sci. Tech.*, 10, 1991, pp 299–300.

Lietuvos.net, Chemical weapon dumping in the Baltic Sea, Lithuanian Website at: lietuvos.net/zinios/gas_ww2.htm.

Lisichkin, GV, Chemical weapons on the seabed, in *Sea-Dumped Chemical Weapons: Aspects, Problems and Solutions*, Ed. AV Kaffka, Kluwer Academic Publishers, Dordrecht, 1996, pp 121–127.

Lotufo, GR, Farrar, JD, Innouye, LS, Bridges, TS and Ringelberg, DB, Toxicity of sediment-associated nitroaromatic and cyclonitramine compounds to benthic invertebrates, *Environmental Toxicology and Chemistry*, 2001, pp 1762–1771.

Malyshev, LP, Technological questions of safe elimination of CW dumps on the Baltic Sea Bed, in *Sea-Dumped Chemical Weapons: Aspects, Problems and Solutions*, Ed. AV Kaffka, Kluwer Academic Publishers, Dordrecht, 1996, pp 93–104.

Manley, RG, Chemical weapon agent and historic chemical munitions disposal: The British experience, in *The Challenge of Old Chemical Munitions and Toxic Armament Wastes*, Ed. T Stock and K Lohs, Sipri Chemical & Biological Warfare Studies, Volume 16, Stockholm International Peace Research Institute/Oxford University Press, 1997, pp 231–240.

Maritime and Coastguard Agency, Report on the wreck of the SS Richard Montgomery, Southampton, November, 2000.

Martens, H, Fonnum, F and Hobraten S, NATO and partner countries study defence-related radioactive and chemical contamination, *NATO Review* 9601-3, No. 1, January 1996, pp 11–16.

Melzian, BD, Zoffmann, C and Spies, RB, Chlorinated hydrocarbons in lower continental slope fish collected near the Farallon Islands, California, *Marine Pollution Bulletin*, No.7, 1987, pp 388–393.

Ministry of Defence, Sea dumping of munitions, undated document.

Ministry of Defence, HMS Royal Oak munition and explosives risk assessment, ES352/97/59, April 1999.

Mitretek Systems, Ocean dumping of chemical weapons, at the Website: http://www.mitretek.org/home.nsf/homelandsecurity/OceanDumpChemWeap, unknown date.

National Report of the Russian Federation, Complex analysis of the hazard related to the captured German chemical weapon dumped in the Baltic Sea, Moscow, 1993.

Nipper, M, Carr, RS, Biedenbach, JM, Hooten, RL, Miller, K and Saepoff, S, Development of marine toxicity data for ordnance compounds, *Archives of Environmental Contamination and Toxicology*, 2001, pp 308–319.

Nottingham, J, The dangers of chemical and biological warfare (CBW), *Ecologist*, 1972, pp 4–6.

O'Connor, TP, Kester, DR, Burt, WV, Capuzzo, JM, Park, PK and Duedall, IW, Waste disposal in the deep ocean: An overview, in *Wastes in the Ocean: Deep Sea Waste Disposal*, Vol. 5, Environmental Science and Technology Series, John Wiley & Sons, pp 3–30.

OSPAR Commission, OSPAR framework for reporting encounters with marine dumped chemical weapons and munitions, 2003, ISBN 1-904426-26-3.

OSPAR Commission, the 2004 update on "Convention-wide practices and procedures in relation to dumped chemical weapons and munitions," 2004, ISBN 1-904426-53-0.

OSPAR Commission, Overview of past dumping at sea of chemical weapons and munitions in the ospar maritime area, 2004 (Revised), ISBN 1-904426-54-9.

OSPAR, Convention for the Protection of the Marine Environment of the North-east Atlantic, Meeting of the Working Group on the Environmental Impact of Human Activities (EIHA), Summary Record, London (Secretariat), 16th-18th November 2004.

Ownby, DR, Belden, JB, Lotufo, GR and Lydy, MJ, Accumulation of trinitrotoluene (TNT) in aquatic organisms: Part 1 – Bioconcentration and distribution in channel catfish (Ictalurus punctatus), *Chemosphere*, 2005, pp 1153–1159.

Paka, V and Spiridonov, M, Research of dumped chemical weapons made by R/V "Professor Shtokman" in the Gotland, Bornholm and Skagerrak dump sites, Eds. T Missiaen, and JP Henriet, *Chemical Munition Dump Sites in Coastal Environments*, 2002, pp. 27–42.

Pearce, KW and Vincent, JD, Investigation into the effects of deep sea pressures on waste materials and disposal containers, AERE Report AERE - M 1254, 1963.

Perera, J, Chemical munitions in the commonwealth of independent states and the surrounding seas, in *The Challenge of Old Chemical Munitions and Toxic Armament Wastes*, Sipri Chemical & Biological Warfare Studies, Volume 16, Ed. T Stock and K Lohs, Oxford University Press, 1997 pp 121–137.

Perera, J and Thomas, A, Fishing boats dodge mustard gas in the Baltic, *New Scientist*, October 1987, p. 24.

Plotnikov, VG, Zamyslov, RA, Surikov, BT, Dobrov, IV and Kayurin OYu, Application of anti-filtering coatings for localisation of toxic warfare chemicals in the Baltic Sea area, in *Sea-Dumped Chemical Weapons: Aspects, Problems and Solutions*, Ed. AV Kaffka, Kluwer Academic Publishers, Dordrecht, 1996, pp 105–107.

Pluck, JA, Munitions dumped in the Atlantic by the UK, MoD memorandum D/ Env Pol/51/2/62 to the Foreign and Commonwealth Office. May 1996.

Plunkett, G, Chemical warfare agent sea dumping off Australia, Department of Defence, Canberra, Australia, Updated 2003, ISBN 0 642 29587 5.

Price, C. and George, R. Ed. by Chappell, M, Environmental Chemistry of Explosives and Propellant Compounds in Soils and Marine Systems, ACS Symposium Series 2012.

Reynders, F, The Coastal Maritime Operations Seminar 2000 and the possible role of NATO in solving the problem of sea-dumped chemical weapons, *The NATO Coastal Maritime Operations Seminar 2000*, pp 157–163.

Riley, JD and Ramster, JW, Woodhead seabed drifter recoveries and the influence of human, tidal and wind factors, *J. Cons. Int. Explor. Mer.*, No. 3, Copenhagen, October 1972, pp 389–415.

Robinson, IS, 'Tidal Vorticity and Residual Circulation', *Deep-Sea Research*, No.3, 1981, pp 195–212.

Sandstrom, J and Forsman, M, Biological degradation of explosives, Abstract, PB 96-121108, ISSN 1104-9154, National Defence Research Establishment, Dept of NBC Defence, Sweden, August 1995.

Searle, WF and Moody, DH, Explosive remnants of war at sea: Technical aspects of disposal, in *Explosive Remnants of War, Mitigating the Environmental Effects*, Ed. AH Westing, Sipri, Taylor & Francis, London, 1985, pp 61–69.

Seltzer, RJ, Ocean pollutants pose potential danger to man, *Chemical and Engineering News*, No.8, 1975, pp 19–20.

Sipri, *World Armaments and Disarmament: Sipri Yearbook 1983*, Preface and Contents, Taylor & Francis, London, 1983.

Soilleux, R, The safe disposal of chemical munitions in the field, *Explosives Engineering*, November 2002, pp 20–23.

Spiess, PN and Sanders, SM, Survey of Chase Disposal Area (NITNATOW), Sponsored by Oceanographer of the Navy through Office of Naval Research, SIO Reference 71-33, 28th December 1971.

Stock, T, Sea-dumped chemical weapons and the chemical weapons convention, in *Sea-Dumped Chemical Weapons: Aspects, Problems and Solutions*, Ed. AV Kaffka, Kluwer Academic Publishers, Dordrecht, 1996, pp 49–66.

Stock, T and Lohs, K (Eds), *The Challenge of Old Chemical Munitions and Toxic Armament Wastes*, Sipri Chemical & Biological Warfare Studies, Volume 16, Stockholm International Peace Research Institute/Oxford University Press, 1997, ISBN 0-19-829190-6.

Stock, T and Lohs, K, Old chemical munitions and warfare agents: Detoxification and degradation, in *The Challenge of Old Chemical Munitions and Toxic Armament Wastes*, Sipri Chemical & Biological Warfare Studies, Volume 16, Ed. T Stock and K Lohs, Oxford University Press, 1997, pp 35–52.

Stub, S, Cross-border environmental problems emanating from defence-related installations and activities, NATO/CCMS/NACC Pilot Study, Summary Final Report, Phase 1 1993–1995, Report No. 206, NATO, April 1995.

Surikov, BT, How to save the Baltics from ecological disaster, in *Sea-Dumped Chemical Weapons: Aspects, Problems and Solutions*, Ed. AV Kaffka, Kluwer Academic Publishers, Dordrecht, 1996, pp 67–70.

Surikov, BT and Duursma, EK, Dumped CW agents in European seas, in *Dumped Chemical Weapons in the Sea – Options*, Ed. EK. Duursma. Published under the auspices of the Dr.A.H.Heineken Foundations for the Environment, 2e Weteringplantsoen 5, 1017 ZD Amsterdam, Netherlands, 1999, ISBN: 90-9012717-8, June 1999, pp 5–10.

Sutton, MA, Dragosits, U, Tang, YS and Fowler, D, Ammonia emissions from non-agricultural sources in the UK, *Atmospheric Environment*, 2000, pp 855–869.

Thorhaug, A, Blake N and Schroeder, PB, The effect of heated effluents from power plants on seagrass (Thalassia) communities quantitatively comparing estuaries in the subtropics to the tropics, *Marine Pollution Bulletin*, 1978, pp 181–187.

Tørnes, JAa, Voie ØA, Ljønes M, Opstad AaM, Bjerkeseth LH and Hussain F, Investigation and risk assessment of ships loaded with chemical ammunition scuttled in Skagerrak, FFI/RAPPORT-2002/04951 Norwegian Defence Research Establishment, 2002.

Townsend, M, The deadly cocktail dumped on our shores, *The Observer*, 19th December 2004.

Trapp, R, *The Detoxification and Natural Degradation of Chemical Warfare Agents*, Sipri Chemical & Warfare Studies, Volume 3, Sipri/Taylor & Francis, London 1985, ISBN 0-85066-309-1.

Underwood, MJ, The effect of the marine environment on the degradation of sea-dumped ammunition, The Royal Military College of Science, 1991 Ammunition Technical Officers Course (Diploma in Explosives Ordnance Technology).

VanDeveer, SD, Protecting Europe's seas: Lessons from the last 25 years, *Environment*, No. 6, July/August 2000, pp 11–26.

van Ham, NHA, Recycling and disposal of munitions and explosives, *Waste Management*, No. 2/3, 1997, pp 147–150.

Volk, F, Reaction products of chemical agents by thermodynamic calculations, in *Sea-Dumped Chemical Weapons: Aspects, Problems and Solutions*, Ed. AV Kaffka, Kluwer Academic Publishers, Dordrecht, 1996, pp 129–143.

Waleij. A, Dumped chemical munition in Skagerrak and the Baltic Sea - an update, Abstract, ISSN 1650-1942, Swedish Defence Research Agency, August 2001.

Weaver, C, Environment report - Old chemical weapons in the Baltic Sea, VOA Special English Environment Report,Broadcast 11th July 2003 http://www/manythings.org/voa/03/030711er_t.htm

White, GF, Snape, JR and Nicklin, S, Bacterial biodegradation of nitrate ester explosives, in *Sea-Dumped Chemical Weapons: Aspects, Problems and Solutions*, Ed., AV Kaffka, Kluwer Academic Publishers, Dordrecht, 1996, pp 145–156.

2. Daily Press Stories – A Generation of Indiscriminate Dumping

Here are some of the chemical weapons of mass destruction the Army dumped into oceans from 1944 to 1970:

http://www.dailypress.com/media/acrobat/2005-10/20226301.pdf [750KB]

Off-shore disposal of chemical agents and weapons conducted by the United States compiled by the U.S. Army Historical Research and Response Team, March 29, 2001

http://www.dailypress.com/media/acrobat/2005-10/20152941.pd [190KB]

Meeting notes: Summary of some chemical munitions sea dumps by the United States, William R. Brankowitz, January 30, 1989

http://www.dailypress.com/media/acrobat/2005-10/20153030.pdf [300KB]

Chemical weapons movement history,William R. Brankowitz, April 27, 1987

http://www.dailypress.com/media/acrobat/2005-10/20152817.pdf [10MB]

http://www.dailypress.com/media/photo/2005-10/20189353.jpg

A barge is loaded with mustard gas canisters that later were thrown somewhere into the Atlantic in 1964.

http://www.dailypress.com/media/photo/2005-10/20189351.jpg

Workers fill the Ralston with mustard gas bombs before its final voyage. The Ralston was sunk in 13,500 feet (4 kilometers) of water.

http://www.dailypress.com/media/photo/2005-10/20189350.jpg

Concrete-encased M55 rockets full of nerve gas are loaded into a ship in 1968 to be scuttled in deep water off New Jersey. The fuel inside the rockets was unstable and tended to spontaneously ignite.

http://www.dailypress.com/media/photo/2005-10/20189349.jpg

Canisters of mustard gas and Lewisite head to sea from California for dumping in 1958.

http://www.dailypress.com/media/photo/2005-10/20189346.jpg

In 1964, mustard gas canisters are pushed into the Atlantic Ocean off New Jersey. Millions of pounds were dumped this way.

http://www.dailypress.com/media/photo/2005-10/20189345.jpg

The SS William Ralston filled with 301,000 mustard gas bombs and 1500, 1-ton canisters of Lewsite sinks in the Pacific off San Fransico in 1958.

http://www.dailypress.com/media/photo/2005-10/20189343.jpg

Chemical warfare agents destined for ocean disposal were often shipped to port via railroad car. This 1958 shipment likely was of Lewisite, a blister agent, and dumped off the coast of South Carolina.

http://www.dailypress.com/media/photo/2005-10/20189342.jpg

Hundreds of dolphins washed ashore in Virginia and New Jersey shorelines in 1987 with burns similar to mustard gas exposure. One marine-mammal specialist suspects Army-dumped chemical weapons killed them.

http://www.dailypress.com/media/photo/2005-10/20189340.jpg

A bomb disposal technician from Dover Air Force Base, Delaware, was burned in 2004 by a mustard gas shell found in a driveway.

http://www.dailypress.com/media/photo/2005-10/20150263.jpg

The samples of ordnance, which were found at former military munitions sites, are placed in a Zapata Engineering trailer at Tidewater Community College, Suffolk, on July 14. In northern Suffolk during the world wars, there was an ordnance dump and processing site called the Nansemond Ordnance Depot (http://www.nao.usace.army.mil/Projects/Nansemond/welcome.html).

The community college, a GE building, some industrial space, and wilderness now stand where the depot once was. But plenty of ordnance was left behind and it is on the federal Superfund list for clean up.

http://www.dailypress.com/media/photo/2005-10/20150262.jpg

The Nansemond Ordnance Depot in Suffolk was used during the world wars to store chemical weapons. It's on the federal Superfund list to clean up leftover ordnance.

http://www.dailypress.com/media/photo/2005-10/20150261.jpg

Zapata Engineering workers look for unexploded ordnance with using handheld magnetometer at General Electric in Suffolk on July 14. In northern Suffolk during the world wars, there was an ordnance dump and processing site called the Nansemond Ordnance Depot. The community college, a GE building, some industrial space, and wilderness now stand where the depot once was. But plenty of ordnance was left behind and it is on the federal Superfund list for clean up.

http://www.dailypress.com/media/photo/2005-10/20150260.jpg

Phil Balvocius uses a magnetometer to look for unexploded ordnance at the former site of an Army munitions depot in Suffolk.

http://www.dailypress.com/media/photo/2005-10/20150258.jpg

Phil Balvocius, a team leader of Zapata Engineering, shows a 40mm ammunition base, which was found at former military munitions sites, at General Electric in Suffolk.

http://www.dailypress.com/media/photo/2005-10/20150257.jpg

Sifter-FNOD-2 -- is looking at the front side of the sifter where the armored front end loader places the suspect munitions contaminated soils on top, and removes the sifted fines that come out the bottom.

http://www.dailypress.com/media/photo/2005-10/20150253.jpg

William Brankowitz, Deputy Project Manager for the U.S. Army Non-Stockpile Chemical Materiel Project, stands next to the containment vessel of the Explosive Destruction System (EDS). The EDS is a transportable treatment system designed to dispose of recovered chemical warfare materiel. The EDS recently treated munitions recovered from the sea in Delaware.

Subject and Site Index